A SECOND CHANCE AT CHANCE AT SUCCESS

A SECOND CHANCE AT SUCCESS

**Remarkably simple ways to turn your
mistakes into opportunities
and open your life to lasting confidence,
happiness and success**

ROB WHITE

illustrations | nicholas kent

Mind Adventure, Inc.
Boston

This book was designed
and produced by:

Mind Adventure, Inc.
49 Forbes Street
Boston, MA 02130
www.mindadventure.com

Production Editor: Nancy Grant Mahoney
Book & Cover Design: Nicholas Kent
Illustrations: Nicholas Kent

ISBN: 978-0-9802299-4-3   0-9802299-4-4

Acknowledgment and Appreciation

I would feel remiss if I didn't acknowledge the work and support of those who helped me make this book possible. I cannot imagine this book coming to completion without the support of a certain few.

My wife, Kat, has put up with a lot over the past couple of years while this book was in progress. I'm thankful she didn't take it personally when I would cancel a dinner date with her because I was absorbed in writing. Kat has influenced my work in many positive ways.

My dear friend, Nicholas Kent, the brilliant and talented artist that created the cover design and illustrations in the book, has supported me strongly, even when I would rave on about some insight or life-lesson that struck me while writing the book.

My editor, Nancy Grant Mahoney, was truly overworked and underpaid for her contributions. I couldn't have done it without her incredible editing assistance to make this book better. She has also become a good friend.

It takes a community to bring a book to the public. It's not a solo effort so, thank you, all of you who have played a part in this mission.

Thank you
Rob White

CONTENTS

Introduction

I began planning this book in the early nineties. It's been two decades in the development phase. During this time, I've learned more about myself and the nature of being a human being than I ever anticipated.

It has become glaringly obvious to me that everyone has incredible potential to succeed. However, we cannot succeed at what we aspire to achieve until we awaken the mind to its creative capacity. The mind must know of what it's capable if it is to waste no energy when in service to the individual's ambitions.

Every individual who succeeds in life, first has to stop

being a problem to himself. You have the power to design your life as you want it to be, but until you learn how you are your own problem, this power is beyond your reach.

 Do you believe that your current lifestyle is the only one possible? What if you truly believed that there is a new world of experiences available and that you already have what it takes to experience it? If you trusted yourself to act in ways that are always in your best interest, what goals would you set?

We live in a world where we are besieged by an enormous collection of negative ideas and opinions. These ideas are continually communicated through what I call the *World Voice*. This voice speaks from the television and the radio; it preaches from the tongues of family, friends, neighbors, work colleagues, and strangers. Its ideas can be read on the internet and in newspapers, magazines, and books.

It's impossible to avoid hearing what the World Voice has to say, and unfortunately, most of its opinions discourage us from believing that life's many riches are for any but the lucky few.

Never disbelieve that you have incredible potential to live as you want to – you do! This is what this book is going to prove to you.

While growing up, I assembled a long list of misleading opinions that discouraged me from believing that my dreams could come true. I remember thinking that the world wasn't nearly as wonderful as I once thought. What's worse is that I assumed these misleading opinions were sound. I had no faith in my own potential to succeed, even when I *felt* I had that potential. How frightening is that?

There was a time in my life when I worried more about avoiding obstacles than about taking advantage of opportunities. When I began to understand that it's not the world that causes me problems, but, rather, it's my own clinging to discouraging opinions, it was like stepping out of a dark cave of confusion and into the bright sunlight of truth. I realized that what I could become was far greater than what I thought. So it was with delight that I began to view my negative opinions as unwanted distractions.

Naturally ambitious

Are you ready for the jolting truth about yourself? One of your great features is that you are *naturally ambitious.* You are endowed with this incredible qual-

ity at birth. Do you know what stops you from expressing this quality? *It's your misperception of yourself.* It's valuable to see how misleading opinions cause negative reactions, which results in a disappointing life.

When you begin seeing yourself rightly, you will find that you are much stronger than your doubts. A truth like this can jolt you free of a thousand wrong ideas you hold about yourself.

At different moments along the path of life, every person has opportunities to be startled awake to the truth about his remarkable potential. These are most encouraging moments. Your dreams are meaningless if you are unaware of your extraordinary ability to make them come true. Just as the strong wings of an eagle are meaningless to the eagle who has forgotten he has them, your potential is useless if you have forgotten you have it.

Curiosity

You are endowed with another incredible quality that enables you to feel in a new and superior way when life challenges you. It's called *curiosity*. The fact that you are reading this book is evidence that you have this quality. Rejoice in your curiosity; you cannot get from where you are to where you want to be in life without it.

Curiosity enables you to correct erroneous opinions that stop you from aspiring higher and living larger. Curiosity has taken human beings from a cave dwelling existence to walking on the moon. It's a costly error to think you can achieve your dreams while suffering with the ache of a doubting mind. A doubting mind quells your curious and ambitious nature.

When you aspire to succeed with a healthy sense of curiosity, you look at life with an inquiring mind. Curiosity is a beautiful thing; without it you cannot gather the facts that support you in your efforts to achieve your aims. Curiosity gives you the power to accomplish far more in far less time.

Facing what's wrong is right

It's not being negative to face the fact that you've been wrong in your assessment of self. In fact, it's being negative to refuse to confront your negative opinions. You open your mind to rightness by confronting wrongness. It is important to understand how wrong ideas harmfully affect you when you refuse to see them as harmful.

If you want to improve the quality of your life, facing what's wrong with your thinking is always the right thing to do. Are you willing to let this book teach you to think in a new way? A resounding, "YES!" is a big step towards extraordinary possibilities.

This book is easy to read and it can have a powerful and positive effect on you. Keep this thought in front of you while reading it. The book even has pictures to help you rise above habitual thinking so you may embrace empowering facts.

When you are willing to admit that *you* attract problems into your life, you will have crossed a bridge and begun your journey to a rich, new world. Are you ready to accept that you need no longer struggle to prove how talented or qualified you are to succeed in life?

You cannot impress a consciousness of success on a mind conditioned by negative opinions. However, when you understand the origin of this negatively conditioned mind, you have the power to stop its incessant motion, the motion that promotes the illusion that you're flawed.

You have the ability to stop the damaging effect of a negative thought-habit. You never lose this ability, although you may not use it. The fuel for taking right action is awareness and the desire to attend to what you can do right for yourself. Yes, you can remove errors of thinking from your mind. Do not shrink away from this truth. It is *you*, and only *you*, who can raise your consciousness above the tyranny of doubting thoughts and fearful opinions. This book will show you how to do this.

What qualifies me?

If you're wondering what qualifies me to write a book of this nature, the answer is simple. I made it a point, several years back, to value the lessons my defeats and failures taught me. I now offer these lessons to you.

If you've looked at your failures with your naturally curious mind and ambitious spirit, and if you've taken time to write down what you've learned, then you too are qualified to write a book like this.

I am offering you a clear look at the struggle between *power* and *doubt* in your mind. My purpose is to help you distinguish between the empowering truth and the misguided opinions that make you doubt yourself. When I learned to separate the two, I was able to make choices and decisions with knowledge that was accurate and right for me. I learned to live authentically.

This book shows you how to access truths that make you eager to set greater challenges and discover your unlimited side. Invariably, I find that when I make decisions and choices from truth, I am able to avail myself of subtle powers of the mind that give me new means of achieving my dreams.

Some personal history

Let me tell you a little about myself. I was born and raised in a small mill town. My early life was influenced by a culture peppered with pessimism and resignation, not uncommon to working class mill towns at the time. It was expected that children would graduate from high school and go to work at one of the two companies that operated mills in the town.

During my preteen years, my confidence could be shaken by even my smallest mistakes. I devoted my efforts to generating excuses for why my life was tough and failure inevitable. My disgruntled mind scoffed at the idea of a beautiful and rich world.

When I was thirteen, something happened that helped me see how my point of view imposed limitations on me. My mother bought me a book that helped me to see things differently. The book was, *How to Win Friends and Influence People*, by Dale Carnegie. After reading this book, I began to understand that if I had a worthy objective, and if I released my mind fully into the objective, a power would well up from deep inside me and carry me to victory. Although I couldn't articulate it then, I could certainly feel it.

I read the book a second and third time and began developing an irrepressible desire for correct thinking from that time forward. I'd never before heard anything like what Dale Carnegie wrote. I began to consider, in a new light, the conversations I'd have with my friends. I could see that we spent a lot of time nourishing disgruntled attitudes. I had learned from Carnegie that the one thing I was going to live with for my entire life, was my attitude, and if my attitude discouraged me, my future would be as grim as my point of view.

Despite my new understanding, I would still fall back on old patterns of thinking. Gradually I became sick and tired of being sick and tired of my life. I wasn't sure what to do about this but I could see that cherishing my beloved complaints about the world was a waste of time. It was difficult to accept this fact, but when I did, the energy I used to blame the world was now available to advance my life.

 To be ignorant of one's ignorance gives power to the ignorance; to be aware of one's ignorance gives power to the self to end the ignorance. It's easy for me to see this with the benefit of hindsight. Hindsight helps us see what our past was really like. By age fifteen, I began consciously slowing the pace of my reactions when with friends. This gave me the opportunity to see circumstances differently.

I can tell you now that a consciousness of success didn't come easy for me. I had to learn to be inspired by my own thinking, not influenced by what my friends had to say. What I eventually learned was that help is always available for the person who is willing to help himself.

During my junior year in high school, I felt a strong urge to put my youthful past behind me and break through to something new. I define my life by epochs, and my first great epoch started when I took control of my life and decided to further my education beyond high school. I began working to save money to go to college, and I became the first member of my family to leave home and attend college.

After working my way through college, I was tempted to play it safe and return to my home town and begin my life as a school teacher. However, I also felt passionate about making my own footprints in new territory. I gave in to this passion and embarked on a new epoch once again.

I moved to a big city by myself, with just sixty dollars in my pocket. I had no job prospects and no contacts in the city. In fact, I'd never been to a city before. After several months of working part time in a grocery store, I secured a teaching position in the public school system, and eventually took on additional responsibilities as the Career Education Coordinator.

It was in this role as teacher and Career Ed Coordinator that I discovered how rarely we use our minds in new ways even though we hope to make a better life for ourselves. So many students would tell me of their dreams of breaking through to a new life, but so few were willing to think in unusual ways. Most would fall back on old thought habits and settle for less.

After seventeen years of teaching, I realized that I too had settled for less. I'd helped many students discover their hidden potential but felt somehow I was not realizing my own. During February break, I decided it was time for a new epoch in my life.

In spite of emphatic calls to 'be reasonable' from family, friends and colleagues,
I gave my notice that this would be my
last year teaching. I gave up my tenured
position, great health plan and retirement fund, to
break into the real estate field with a goal of building
a million-dollar business.

This new epoch was an exciting new beginning for
me. New beginnings are available whenever we mus-
ter the courage to break free from old paradigms to
reach for something of greater value. It means we prefer growth to stagnation. Can you think of anything
more inspiring?

Over the next decade, I built a real estate development business with projects on the east and west
coasts. I even got involved in developing restaurants
and was successful with that endeavor. It didn't come
easy, but I'd mastered the art of believing in myself
even in tough times, and this I pass on to you.

If you are willing to look beyond the mental boundaries that limit your life and if you are willing to bear
the confusion of not having all the answers, you will
find answers in this book. Your opportunity to see

the difference between inspiring truths and misleading opinions is here, right now; go after it right now. Keep reading.

I consider this my greatest epoch yet, sharing with you the knowledge I've gathered from my personal life-lessons. When we share, we plant opportunities for those with which we share as well as for ourselves. This is an act of true human consideration. Everyone wins. It's the Golden Rule, the Law of Reciprocity, in action. Nothing is more beautiful than sharing and receiving more of what we've shared.

The fact that you are still reading indicates that you are ready to dismiss any attitude that will stop you from living a richer life. I am offering you a way out, and remember – this is coming from a person who, at one time, was fiercely devoted to arguing in favor of the proposition that, *Life is tough, and the best you can do is cope.*

It's amazing! We make the world what it is and then complain about it or rejoice in it. If you're ready to make a world that will have you rejoicing, prepare yourself to meet an extraordinary part of you - the part which is free of doubts and fears.

Sensible course

You are about to embark on a journey towards success. Consider this book your guide. It offers a sensible course of action that helps you take the raw stuff of circumstance and turn it into healthy opportunities for flourishing in all areas of your life.

Your curiosity and natural ambition together create a dynamic force. When channeled rightly, this force demolishes any consciousness of lack that stops you from accomplishing your dreams.

I am not trying to reform you but, rather, to awaken you to your superlatively creative nature. However, I cannot do this without your help. It matters not where you're starting from; it's how ambitious and curious you're willing to be that will determine how far you'll go.

Don't resist the opportunity that stands before you. It's a glorious day when you accept that you cannot afford to be who you were yesterday, not if you intend to experience a different tomorrow. Nothing but your own resistance is keeping you from living your dreams. Are you ready to resolve the inner contradictions that are holding you back? I can show you how, but you have to do the work.

Take time to pause and reflect when you come upon an exercise or process; feel free to modify it, if necessary, so it works for you. Walt Whitman said, "You have not known what you are, you have slumbered upon yourself all your life." Come - allow me to help you awaken from any deep slumber you're in when it comes to the incredible truth about you. This book is offered in a spirit of goodwill; relax and enjoy the adventure.

ONE

Ask Healthy Questions

Operation Wonder

Your mind is meant to serve you; you own it, it doesn't own you; at least it's not supposed to. A great way to monitor your mind's internal conversation is to pay attention to your inward self-talk. When you talk to yourself, what are your favorite topics of conversation? Do you simply replay the hand-me-down conversations that come from the World Voice, or are you thinking for yourself?

Does your inward self-talk disparage your inspiring daydreams or encourage them? If you're to take mastery of your life, you must take possession of your mind. You do this by making it a prime principle of your life to think intelligently for yourself.

A great way to think intelligently is to engage in a process that I call *Operation Wonder*. Engaging in *Operation Wonder* requires the willingness to question everything you believe. This means you must consciously refuse to go along with old negative thought-habits, just because they've been around forever. There is a part of you, right now, that is saying "YES!" to this suggestion; can you feel it? *Operation Wonder* is a right course of action because you're a curious being.

When you engage in *Operation Wonder,* you choose to listen to your authentic voice, not to thought-voices that parrot the opinions of others. Your authentic

voice knows what is best for you, and it always speaks the truth. Stay with this choice, even when the World Voice shouts loudly, trying to interfere with your mental affairs.

Successfully engaging in *Operation Wonder* requires that you value being teachable more than you value the bogus self-satisfaction of defending old points of view. It is amazing how attached we become to old thoughts and views.

It takes courage to challenge old opinions that we preciously hold as valid. Challenging them can leave us feeling deserted and helpless. We find ourselves asking, "*What am I to think next?*" When we are open to fresh opinions, it becomes apparent that a lot of our current self-talk is nonsense.

Simple acceptance of the fact that our self-talk is on the wrong track enables us to correct it. Dare to look at the mental boundaries you've imposed upon yourself. Begin asking healthy questions; that is the key element of *Operation Wonder*. It's a lot of fun, and astonishing insights will come.

The more you question the validity of your discouraging points of view, the quicker you rescue yourself from self-limiting beliefs masquerading as truths. *Operation Wonder* attracts healthy answers that empower you.

You turn down the volume on negative self-talk when you think of it as nothing but bad thought-habits that need to be broken.

Student: *What do I do to engage in* Operation Wonder?

Teacher: *Starting now, pledge not to be held hostage by discouraging thought-voices that haunt you. Value your growth and development more than the false sense of security you got from old self-talk that discourages you from exploring anything new.*

Do you want to get all that you can from this book? Engage in *Operation Wonder* while reading every page.

Honest self-facing

Have you ever noticed how you unwittingly victimize yourself with opinions that make you feel inadequate or insecure? Would you like to know the cause of

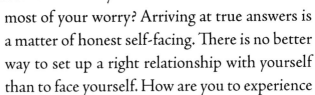

most of your worry? Arriving at true answers is a matter of honest self-facing. There is no better way to set up a right relationship with yourself than to face yourself. How are you to experience

your unrealized potential if you don't feel right
within yourself?

Take a moment now and commit to yourself:
"I am here to grow, and nothing will block my goal."
Say it again, like you mean it. *"I am here to grow, and
nothing will block my goal."* One more time, *"I am here
to grow, and nothing will block my goal."* Say it until it
feels rejuvenating.

You'd be surprised at how practiced you have
become at the art of self-evasion by avoiding
responsibility for your personal growth and
development. Why do we avoid self-confrontation?
Because self-confrontation forces us to face the truth
about cherished thought-habits that make bearable
our lives of struggle and confusion. When practicing
self-evasion, we come up with clever excuses to avoid
discovering our capacity to win at the game of life.

May I ask you a healthy question? Is it wise to insist
that you are right about self-limiting opinions that
slam shut the door to your potential? Honest self-facing can be a startling wake-up call. There is no better
way to reach the remarkable truth about your unlim-

ited potential than to accept that you've been wrong about your excuses for not succeeding. Self-evasion is the nemesis of self-fulfillment. It's that simple.

> **Teacher:** *Do you know what happens when you realize what's wrong with your current opinions about yourself and take responsibility for them?*
>
> **Student:** *What?*
>
> **Teacher:** *You gain the inner strength to change.*

The making of thought-habits

Whenever you repeat a thought over time and act as though that thought were true, you create a thought-habit. Thought-habits become beliefs. Beliefs have the power to make your choices and decisions for you.

Thought-habits are beliefs.

Do you know why you become dependent on thought-habits? Because they comfort you and excuse you from the obligation to explore anything new. Unfortunately, when you become comfortable with a thought-habit, you accept its logic, even if it is untrue and can harm you.

When your thought-habits motivate you to be flexible, and inspire you to act in ways that enrich your life, there's no reason to question them. For most folks, however, this is not often the case.

The typical mind is full of erroneous thought-habits that throw a damp blanket on enthusiasm. These thought- habits voice themselves when a person dares to daydream about a life beyond the ordinary. The thought-voices excuse failure, making it very uncomfortable to step beyond the limits of one's comfort zone.

Am I saying that we knowingly value failure and willingly accept it? Certainly not! However, erroneous thought-habits destroy our faith in ourselves, thus impairing our ability to reason rightly. The most baffling question is why it takes so long to realize this. The answer is quite simple. We are tempted to feel friendly toward all habits of thought, be they positive or negative, because we fear being with nothing if we're not. Being with 'no thought' actually can be very empowering, but most of us believe it's a weak position to take.

If you are to actualize your loftiest dreams, then you must endure the discomfort of challenging that collection of discouraging thoughts that you've developed into habits. But get ready! They will fight back in every way to maintain their dominance over you.

Healthy answers

Healthy questions attract healthy answers. Healthy answers rescue you from your misunderstandings. Do you want to discover marvelous things about yourself? Begin by appreciating the part of you that delights in what you are reading right now. This part of you loves to ask healthy questions. It is the curious and ambitious part of you, the authentic part of you.

Healthy answers focus your mind on what's right about life and what's right about you. There is no person to whom the truth is not available. Any feeling that you hold about your problems being permanent is due to a misunderstanding. Such feelings encourage an unhealthy attitude.

Healthy answers enable you to deal with your problems from an optimistic perspective. Healthy answers give you the power to lift yourself above harmful, unhealthy attitudes. They are a source of strength. They contribute to a feeling of being in control. They help you realize that when it comes to your life, you are the commander in chief, not your mind. It's wonderfully liberating to experience this realization.

When misleading opinions control your attitude, you feel trapped. "One great thought breathed into a man may regenerate him." - William Ellery Channing. Great thoughts come from healthy questions.

Healthy answers come when you examine the opinions that make you feel flawed. Such opinions are flawed, not you! Ask yourself, "Are these opinions valid? Am I in possession of all the facts? Is there something that I do not understand?" Ask with a deep desire for the truth and you will attract healthy answers.

Illuminating Tip: Misunderstandings energize discouraging thought-habits, and discouraging thought-habits protect misunderstandings from being challenged.

What will you lose if you let go of misunderstandings that insist that your problems are permanent? You will lose the false sense of security you get from leaning on the crutch of the old and familiar. You will lose your negative attitude. So, you will lose nothing and you will gain access to fabulous possibilities. Say, "YES!" to that.

A principal peril

It's a principal peril to close one's eyes and stick one's head in the sand like the ostrich when the lion is approaching. The ostrich thinks that denying the fact of the lion will save him from the tooth and the claw. Things cannot go right until we stop clinging to our wrong points of view. We stop clinging when we ask healthy questions.

It's plain and simple: Healthy questions help you sustain a healthy attitude in even the most difficult times, and a healthy attitude helps you value what is truly valuable – healthy answers. Sweet liberty!

 Dr. Seuss was rejected by twenty-seven publishing houses when he submitted his first book. President Ulysses S. Grant failed as a store clerk, a farmer, and a real estate agent. Thomas Edison was dyslexic and nearly deaf. Wouldn't you love to know the healthy questions these folks asked to overcome their adversities.

You were speaking with a two hundred-word vocabulary by age two, a ten thousand-word vocabulary by six. Some of you learned to swim by age one. Most of you mastered reading within a year of trying. Wouldn't you love to know the healthy questions you unconsciously asked yourself during this incredible growth period in your life.

It's never a matter of IQ, sex, race, creed, religion, education or political affiliation that determines your place in history; it's always a matter of facing the unfamiliar, and asking healthy questions.

Nothing is trivial

You may think that it's only important to ask healthy questions about matters of substance. The truth is that you must learn to respond rightly in situations both trivial and substantial by making a habit of asking healthy questions in all matters. Nothing is trivial.

Healthy questions advance your life in all situations.

I'm going to tell on myself. I remember setting out to buy a new car. The salesperson proceeded to tell me what everyone was buying that year. I told him that I didn't want him to influence me; I wanted to decide for myself. I proceeded to ask him questions that were important to me. I ended up purchasing a car from a dealer across the street.

The above experience made something very clear to me. I weaken my resolve to think for myself when I let others make decisions for me. If I make this a habit, I begin doubting my very ability to make intelligent decisions. This is very demoralizing.

A week after purchasing the car, which turned out to be the perfect car for me, I went to buy some running shoes. The salesperson was pushing one brand of famous footwear, even though I liked the feel of another. He was very persistent. I asked a few questions, smiled, shook my head, and purchased the brand I preferred. I loved the shoes I bought.

The above experiences helped me to understand that the biggest obstacle to nurturing my own decisive mind is allowing others to decide for me. This is true when it comes to deciding something as important as buying the right car, or as simple as buying shoes.

Do you understand?

Do you now understand that you do not already understand everything there is to understand about you? Any day that you are willing to abandon the false comfort of old familiar answers by asking new questions, is a great day. Rejoice in knowing that there is so much more of you to explore. Venture into the unknown. Engage in *Operation Wonder*. Ask healthy questions.

Let's move on. It's time to look at a human experience that's unavoidable ... NO, NO, NO!

TWO

60,000 NO's

The two-letter word that makes grown men tremble

There is a two-letter word that has been masquerading as helpful for thousands of years but, in truth, is harmful. The word is NO. Most guilt, blame, and shame come from hearing NO, NO, and NO! This one word can make grown men tremble.

When NO is spoken with an angry tone, it makes us feel insecure, especially when accompanied by ridicule or a contemptuous remark. The consequences of NO are dire, and though they may be subtle at first, they gain strength over time.

A mind assaulted by an onslaught of NO's loses its edge and grows dull. Most people are unaware of the corrosive damage that NO's cause in their lives. Understanding will help you lift yourself above this negative conditioning. Is this something you'd like to do?

Sweet silence

I wish I could bring you back to the sweet silence of the womb where NO did not exist. During the first three months in the womb, you grew from a tiny speck into a four-inch long, living being. By seven months, you'd developed eyes and were able to cry. Imagine what would have happened if you'd heard, "NO, NO, NO! *Stop moving! Stop kicking!*" We could have incredible power available if we lived in a world without NO.

In the sweet silence of the womb, there is no self-doubt. When you exited the dark safety of the womb and entered the harsh light of the hospital room, you were turned upside down, slapped on your butt, and your life-sustaining umbilical connection to mom was severed. However, your mind was still a NO-Free

Zone, so you managed these trials of birth with the same vitalizing strength that you managed the unimaginable changes you endured in the womb.

Unfortunately, the world is not NO-Free. By age two, when you began exploring, the NO's began coming. No one can avoid them. Mom forbids you from exploring for your own safety. *"NO, don't touch the plug!"* *"NO, NO, don't play with the scissors!"* Mom repeats what she heard her mom say when she did those things. *"NO!"* Indeed, mom says, *"NO,"* for your own good – but it doesn't feel good to you.

I once read that children are exposed to 60,000 NO's between the ages of two and six. It's difficult to remain curious and ambitious in the face of this onslaught. What is to become of a child if he loses his curiosity? Yet it seems an unsolvable dilemma, how to keep a child safe in the absence of NO.

A dark shadow

Every small child has a sense of his immense potential. However, by the time the child hears his first one thousand NO's, he's already beginning to feel unsure about himself and insecure about life. He soon learns that whenever he tests his potential, there's a NO lurking about. It only takes a dozen NO-Experiences before the child feels like a dark shadow is following him every time he tries something new.

By age four, when the child hears a NO of any nature, he suffers physical strain. His heart rate quickens as he cringes at the prospect of being punished. That peaceful state of being that he experienced in the womb is now the exception, rather than the rule.

 When I was in first grade, I was told a hundred times, "NO, *don't try to pet the neighbor's cat; it will scratch you.*" The more I heard NO, the more I wanted to pet the cat. One morning while I was leaving for school, the cat passed by. I decided to pick it up. I'd barely bent over when I heard a scream from the neighbor's kitchen window, "*NO, NO, NO!*"

I ran off to school feeling guilty, sure that I was going to get it when I got home. I had a knot in my stomach all day. Nothing came of it, but I still remember this NO-Moment. Am I still living under the tyranny of this old NO?

What insight might help you get over your touchiness around NO and grant you what you need in order to grow? Notice, as you continue to read, how much more nervousness is brought on by your fear of NO than by the NO itself.

As the child grows, the NO's grow in force and number. In your pre-teen and teen years, the NO's take new forms: ridiculing remarks, mocking gestures, teasing, bullying, sarcasm, and social rejection. NO, NO, NO, NO, NO and NO! By young adulthood, we are already paying a heavy price for suffering so many NO's.

It's much easier to deal with life when you look at it without referencing past NO's. Are you beginning to feel suspicious of the NO's that have duped you into feeling insecure? This will make complete sense to you as you proceed.

The harming effect of NO

Every person feels some sense of inadequacy in some area of life, be it athletics, business, social affairs, public speaking, money matters, love relationships, etc. These feelings are a consequence of NO's being interpreted incorrectly.

Childhood NO's are the cause of adult fears of criticism; they are the cause of adults feeling helpless when facing something unusual or challenging. Some NO's are more damaging than others.

NO's don't just come and go, they linger, sometimes for a lifetime. Let this statement alert you to the NO's that linger in your mind. We all come to wrong conclusions about ourselves when hearing NO's in our childhood. We proceed to create a false version of ourselves from false conclusions we make when we hear NO, a version of self that is flawed and helpless.

This false version of self is the *Counterfeit Self*. I've dedicated a full chapter to this later in the book. The *Counterfeit Self* shackles you to the false conclusions that you drag through your life, like a prisoner dragging a ball and chain.

Are you tired of the mental torture that comes from childhood NO's? Great! Let's look deeper into how you are unknowingly persecuted by them and show you how to escape this persecution.

I still hear echoes of old NO's when trying something new, but because I understand the nature of NO, they no longer wreak havoc with my feelings. This is a desirable state of mind.

The creation of the deep subconscious

I have a theory that the subconscious is like a basement, created by the mind to hide the NO's from our consciousness. When NO's assault us, they become overwhelming, so the mind suppresses them by burying them deep in its basement. Perhaps that is why we call it the deep, dark subconscious.

Well, it's time to grab your coal miner's hat with the light on top. It's time to shine the light of truth on your hiding place of NO's. It's time to learn how to free yourself of the fear and doubt they bring you.

When you shine the light of truth on any given NO, you realize that the only power it has is the power you give it. Let this truth become clear to you. Truth can conquer false constraints that you've unwittingly imposed upon yourself.

> *Truth can conquer false constraints that you've unwittingly imposed upon yourself.*

The next time a NO rises from the deep basement of your mind, recognize it for what it is – nothing but the wailing specter of old criticisms and long-gone failures. It's an explosion of suppressed energy that gets its power from the attention you pay it.

Declare your independence

Understanding the crippling nature of NO is liberating. Let this understanding be the foundation of your declaration of independence from the intimidation of old NO's. I did myself tremendous good when I realized how susceptible I was to the flimsy power of this word.

Your mind's ability to conceive of a rewarding future is crippled by old NO's that echo in its dark chambers. A mind that works undisturbed by NO's, is not only able to conceive of a rewarding future, it's able to achieve it.

A mind that works undisturbed by NO's, is not only able to conceive of a rewarding future, it's able to achieve it.

You cannot discover the bright, beautiful truth about your immense potential until you believe in yourself. You cannot believe in yourself while under the influence of NO. Great achievers achieve things of great value when they are not under the influence of NO.

Even helpful NO's can feel harmful

Certainly some NO's are essential to basic safety: "NO, don't cross the road without looking both ways." "NO, don't eat that, it's a moth ball!"

The word NO is meant to be helpful when used to warn of legitimate danger or guide us to safer behavior. However, even helpful NO's cause painful reactions when we become sensitive to NO. Now every NO takes its toll.

When we're sensitive to NO's, they bite with a venom that poisons our confidence. That's because they trigger feelings of incompetence. A person sensitized to NO, will avoid trying anything new because he fears the pain of reprimand that comes with failing. This 'fear of criticism' is a crippling fear that stirs up unpleasant memories, which distract the mind from imagining a successful future.

The person who fears criticism loses the ability to distinguish helpful NO's from harmful ones. He becomes timid in the face of any NO, and cannot grow.

You now know where the echoes of NO come from. You also know that these echoes dampen your ambitious spirit and curious nature. You need not tolerate them. However, if you intend to grow, it's important to recognize when a NO is offering an important lesson.

My father would say, "*NO, NO! I've told you a thousand times – don't play with my cigarette lighter.*" He said NO for my well-being but he said it with a harsh tone. I concluded that there was something wrong with me; after all, my father was playing with the cigarette lighter constantly.

When sensitive to NO, we come to one of two conclusions:

(1) There's something wrong with me.

(2) There's something wrong with the world, and I'm its victim.

Both conclusions trigger emotional reactions that make us feel helpless. You must believe these facts about your relationship with NO.

Howling sound of NO

By the time NO has made its first one thousand appearances, it has begun to howl through the chambers of your mind. The howl is not part of your original nature. I urge you to believe this. You advance more quickly when you do.

NO's are influences that come from other minds. However, you create the howling in your own mind. If you create it, then you have the power to destroy it. You already know the way to begin – ask healthy questions.

 Howling NO's stifle your ability to imagine a better tomorrow because they destroy your sense of self-reliance today. Henry David Thoreau spoke of men leading lives of quiet desperation. I believe howling NO's are the cause of this desperation.

Here's a healthy question: When your mind is a haunted house of howling NO's, how can you possibly grow? You may wish that you had the courage to explore, but when opportunity knocks, you lock the door. This is certainly a desperate condition.

When echoing NO's would possess my mind, I was most concerned with not looking foolish. I'd do whatever I could to avoid being criticized. I'd lower my expectations rather than suffer the humiliation. I thought I was retreating from danger but I was retreating from life.

When I learned to dismiss echoing NO's as meaningless, my daydreams became a luminous display of exciting adventures, and I dared to act on them. As I mentioned in the introduction, when I decided to quit teaching to begin a new epoch in my life, family and friends all said, "*NO, NO, NO! Are you crazy?*"

My ambitious nature said, *"It's time to break out; it's time for something new."* I've done wonderfully well with my new endeavors. Would I have, had I allowed the NO's of my friends to take root in my head?

Born free

It's because you were born free of NO that you are able to dream big. *"I want to be an astronaut; oh wait … I want to be a rodeo clown; wait, wait … I want to be a sky diver."*  There was nothing to stop your mind from dreaming of soaring.

Napoleon Hill said, "Whatever the mind can conceive and believe, it can achieve." The key word is *believe*. It's impossible to believe what the mind conceives when howling NO's demolish your confidence.

When the mind is penned-in with NO's, we begin believing that life is tough and that we're powerless to do anything about it. A feeling of resignation sinks in, and with it comes a dull ache of longing. I imagine it's what a wild horse feels when penned in a corral. I met a horse trainer who said that no matter how much you train a wild horse, he still yearns to run free. The trainer believed that if a trained horse could speak, it would say, "*My life will never be as good as it was when I ran free.*"

 When feeling free, we run and play joyfully, no matter what our age. When our mind is penned-in with NO's, there's an enormous chasm between the life we experience and the life we once conceived.

Do you feel that dull ache of longing in any domain of your life? What do you think stops you from achieving those lofty dreams you once conceived? Do you think life stops you? The next time you feel that life is stopping you, look again. Right there you will find a howling NO from your past. Old NO's triggering memories of past failures and pain – that's the problem!

Understanding is power when used to end self-deception. You are deceiving yourself when you doubt that you have what it takes to succeed. Self-doubt is baseless when backed by nothing but howling NO's.

Illuminating Tip: You can stop yourself from being victimized by howling NO's.

Psychological crimes

Psychological crimes of the mind are the worst kind; they cause emotional problems that are harmful to the individual. Furthermore, when these psychological crimes are severe, they often manifest outwardly as social crimes that are harmful to humankind. Howling NO's cause psychological crimes. They assault you with opinions that make you feel deficient and defective. They make you tremble with fear at the prospect of starting something new.

When old NO's detect the slightest doubt, they begin howling and play a slick trick on you. They pretend they are coming to help but in fact, they cripple your enthusiasm and weaken your resolve to succeed, putting you in dire psychological straits. Dare to believe what you're reading.

Illuminating Tip: Howling NO's commit psychological crimes in your mind.

Whosoever wants to free his mind of NO can do so. It's time for a healthy question. *What great achievement does NO have to its credit that entitles it to discourage you when you're contemplating something new?* Here's a tip: No longer allow yourself to be snowed by NO.

Can angry wolves, howling on a movie screen, harm you? Well, calmly see the insanity of being intimidated by NO's howling in your mind. The next time they howl, pause and cooly say, *"It's only my misunderstanding mind that has me listening to these NO's. There's no valid reason for me to tremble when I hear the howls."* Mean it when you say it. Say it aloud. You are saying it to gain a better perspective, to see through the deceptive nature of howling NO's.

It's one thing to listen to advice of caution from a correctly reasoning mind. It's quite another thing to allow old NO's to dull the sharp edge of your curious nature.

Learn not to burn

There's a firefighter's program in Tennessee called *Learn Not To Burn.* It teaches children how to survive fires. The statement, *Learn not to burn,* is a great motivator. You're now learning how not to burn from NO.

You learn not to burn from howling NO's when you learn all you can about their deceitful nature. NO's burn when they cause emotional upsets ranging from mild worry to extreme nervous tension. The damaging emotional effect of NO grows as the echoes grow.

A great way to learn not to burn from NO's is to stop using the word to burn others. Wipe it out of your vocabulary. Be creative. Replace it with a word that empowers you to make necessary changes.

When I set out to omit the word NO from my vocabulary, I was startled to discover how often I used it. It became clear to me that if I insisted on living in a world of NO's, I could expect to be burnt by them. What I put out there has to come back; it's simply the Law of Attraction in action. Perhaps it's better understood as a matter of sowing and reaping. There are universal laws that are immutable, so it's best to work with them. I will speak of these often throughout the book.

Do you think I'm making too much of the matter of NO? All ideas that make you feel inferior for any reason, are obstructions to your growth and development. Most such ideas come from old NO's howling. Can you afford to ignore this?

The Curse of NO

Right sight gives you mental strength. A great way to set your sight right is to investigate the curse of NO.

After hearing a thousand NO's, you unknowingly set up a NO-Center in the basement of your mind. This center is highly emotionalized. This NO-Center curses you.

When NO's gain control, you fall under their spell and begin believing what's *not* true about you. You believe that you're incapable of making your dreams come true. This belief curses you.

Howling NO's flock together to use your creative energy in destructive, not constructive, ways. Dependency on NO is slavery to feelings of insufficiency. This feeling curses you.

Look into the eyes of someone who is cursed by NO – there is no glow. Under the curse of NO, he feels helpless, resentful, and even angry. All are a consequence of feelings of insufficiency brought on by, "NO, NO, NO!" Had this person never been exposed to NO, he'd eagerly learn, naturally grow, and his eyes would glow.

The feeling of intimidation brought on by NO is harmful to your mental health and physical well-being. Learn to value this truth above all else. Lift the curse!

Consequences of the NO-Curse

There are many consequences to being cursed by NO. First and foremost, you become a *NO-it-all*; you look at life from a discouraging point of view and you reinforce this viewpoint by insisting you know all there is to know. You say NO to anything that's encouraging.

When caught in the role of *NO-it-all*, you choose protection over correction. You protect your distressing position by saying NO to helpful suggestions. A *NO-it-all* is a know-it-all that denies himself the opportunity to learn anything new.

When caught in the role of NO-it-all, you choose protection over correction.

St. Bernard of Clairvaux said, "Nothing can work me damage except myself; the harm that I sustain, I carry about with me, and never am a real sufferer but by my own fault." The fault lies in being a *NO-it-all*.

NO-it-alls acquire a strange need for gloom and doom; they feel compelled to stare at old NO's, and what one stares at, stares back! Stare at NO's and you have *NO-Attacks*.

NO-Attacks are another consequence of the NO-Curse. A howling NO can pounce from anywhere, like a purse-snatcher that attacks unexpectedly. However, an attacking NO steals something much more valuable than money. Attacking NO's are energy thieves that weaken your resolve by stealing your creative energy.

NO-Attacks interfere with life's natural flow. They cause emotional strain. This has a deleterious effect on every aspect of your life from limiting your income to destroying your health. It's not what life hands you that determines your destiny but, rather, how you deal with attacking NO's.

NO-Attacks *interfere with life's natural flow.*

When the NO-Curse prevails, you soon find yourself *NO-Stuck*. When *NO-Stuck*, you're shackled to memories of past failures and cannot see beyond your own nose. These memories, be they conscious or unconscious, have you stuck right where you stand; the world becomes an intimidating place in which to live. Hesitating and procrastinating are the behavioral symptoms of this condition.

When NO-Stuck, you cannot see beyond your nose.

Old NO's connect to each other, like the links of a chain. When an experience pulls down the link of an old NO, many more links come tumbling after and into your mind. Let this image help you understand.

The *NO-Stuck* condition thwarts all ambition; it causes a dreadful drain of constructive energy. Now the *NO-Stuck* person believes that quitting is the intelligent move. The best he can do is make a feeble attempt to achieve his ambition and when he fails, he can point to this effort as evidence of how stacked life is against him.

> *NO-Stuck is the condition of mind that has one believing that quitting is the intelligent move.*

Being *NO-Stuck* is a matter of mental mechanics. When the mind plays and replays the same scenes of failure, the consequences are predictable. *NO-Stuck* puts you on a collision course with failure. The mind can only project what it knows, and when it's *NO-Stuck*, all it knows is NO. Now it stops looking for answers.

> *The mind can only project what it knows, and when NO-Stuck, all it knows is NO.*

It's time to let go. Any advice offered by NO, robs you of your resourcefulness. You need only be ready to let go and you do it by asking healthy questions. Healthy questions attract resourceful answers. Become enthusiastic about what you are reading.

How do you do that?

Self-sabotage is the inevitable result of long term involvement with NO. It's time to have some fun. Imagine teaching someone how you manage to sabotage yourself when facing a new challenge. How do you do that?

Here's how I do it. When wrongly involved with NO, I overuse the word 'cannot'. Have you given any thought to the word 'cannot'? It's saying that I CAN not-do something. I'm insisting that I CAN do whatever it takes to be sure that I will NOT do what needs doing. This statement of apparent weakness is actually a statement of strength: I am saying "*NO!*" to doing it, and am committed to proving that the statement, "*I CANnot!*" is true.

I'm a genius at proving I CANnot do something when I declare it so. What do I say to prove I CANnot do it? I say, "*I couldn't do it in the past, so why should now be any different.*" What emotion do I stir up? I get resentful if someone insists that I could do it. What tone of voice do I use? I mutter gruffly, "*I CANnot! do it.*" How do I stand? I stand tall and proud, like a silverback gorilla pounding his chest, but I pound my chest in the name of NO. What expression do I set on my face? I wear a grimace that would discourage even the most optimistic of motivators.

Now let's turn the spotlight on you. Describe to yourself what you do to prove that you CANnot do something. Speak about yourself as if you were someone else. Doing this helps you realize the power you wield in your life. The more you understand what you do to feel helpless, the easier it is to break the bad habit.

Everyone makes the passage

This is extraordinary self-work you are doing right now. Everyone passes through a series of shock waves when first assaulted by NO. But now you know that you don't have to suffer the assault forever.

You can break the back of *NO-Stuck* patterns. You are not obligated to take NO's imprudent advice. NO's tell you that retreating from life protects you. This nonsense disguised as wisdom makes you feel like a loser. Don't listen.

You are at that place, in your passage through life, where it's time to stop saying, "I CANnot." Stop pledging your allegiance to NO. If you weren't ready, you'd not be reading this book. Unless you stop identifying with NO, you will never know the whole of you.

You now know the slick, dirty tricks that NO's play on you. You know that when NO's detect the slightest weakness, they pounce and smother your confidence. When you first heard the word 'NO', you were innocent and vulnerable. You've grown up, your body has changed; yet the NO's remain the same. Your new spirit of self-change will send them away.

I believe psychosomatic illnesses are a consequence of old NO's. They cause tension headaches and depression. They disturb one's restful sleep. They turn 'love of life' into 'fear of life.' When you stop reacting to a howling NO in the usual way, you begin doing what is right for you. Notice the curious feeling you are now awakening to.

Let's delve deeper. There's more to look at before you can act in ways that will give you lasting victory over all those NO's.

Taunting NO's give power to the enslaving attitude of WOE ......

THREE

From NO to WOE

Mental Karma

I believe in *mental karma*. I believe that what's done in the realm of thinking duplicates its tone in the realm of feelings and then expresses itself in the world of action. Karma is simply the Universal Law of Cause and Effect in action. In other words, the sum of your beliefs and strongly held opinions determines your attitude, mood, and disposition. And these govern your responses to life. I call this process, *mental karma.*

Certainly, the idea of a thought begetting a feeling and a feeling begetting an action is not new. *Mental karma* proves this to you in a thousand ways, every day. Even the expression on your face is telling. It reveals whether you are under the spell of an old NO or are feeling confident and free. This expression is a simple example of *mental karma* having its effect on you.

Mental karma is of stupendous value when correctly used. When you know your own mind and are faithful to your intentions, you control your *mental karma* and are in command of your destiny.

You already know the karmic effect of allowing NO to repeatedly torment you – you hesitate and procrastinate to the point where it puts you in a woeful emotional state. Rather than saying, *"If it is to be it is up to me."* you wail out, *"WOE is me, what am I to do?"* You then forsake your dreams by doing what a woeful emotional state requires of you – whine and blame.

 How can wailing out, *"WOE is me,"* ever create a positive karmic effect? It cannot. How are you to express yourself in new and promising ways with an inner thought-voice that's wailing,

"*WOE is me!*"? This harmful voice can only aggravate your already agitated condition. The Law of Cause and Effect always prevails.

The more aware you are of what drives you to act as you do, the easier it is to make productive corrections. You create a marvelous opportunity when you recognize a negative tendency and deal with it without woeful self-condemnation. This is about being able to observe the flawed self dispassionately and to recognize the woeful attitude that causes despair and gets in the way of the psychological repair.

If you're to become the prime cause of the effects in your life, and if you're to lift yourself above adverse internal conditions to effect real productive change, then you must create a new relationship with adverse circumstances. "It lies in our own power to attune the mind to cheerfulness." - Berthold Auerbach.

Whenever you respond to adverse external circumstances with an inner voice wailing, "WOE," your ability to work through the matter is badly compromised. *Mental karma* demands this.

What On Earth

WOE is my acronym for, **What On Earth**. When someone laments, *"WOE is me,"* or anything of that nature, he is saying, *"What On Earth is causing my problems?"* He's blaming the world for what's happening to him.  This whining attitude casts him directly in the role of helpless victim. The only reason his activities in the world are ineffective is because the activity in his mind is woefully defective.

When WOE dominates one's inward self-talk, excuse-making becomes the salient feature of his personality. It's a matter of being *No-Stuck* and converting it to *WOE-Stuck*. That's *mental karma*.

WOE is a distressing attitude. It comes with strong, but wrong, beliefs about lack and limit. WOE decimates our ambitious nature by putting us in a rut — we miss new opportunities today because we are busy lamenting the lost opportunities of yesterday. I believe WOE is a man-made devil that has us fearing everything.

When WOE is in control, the mind becomes susceptible to more and more *NO-Attacks*. They roll in like stormy ocean waves, flooding the mind with negative emotions, which further dampen the spirit.

Just as you can be *NO-Stuck,* you can be *WOE-Stuck.* In fact, being *NO-Stuck* leads to being *WOE-Stuck.* How do you know when you're *WOE-Stuck?* You find yourself asking, *"Why does life hurt so much?"* This question assumes that sadness of WOE is permanent; it's begging for wrong answers.

Student: *"Why does WOE hurt so much?"*

Teacher: *"It's obvious that you're doing something wrong. When you take responsibility for correcting it, the pain will subside."*

Where does WOE come from? I believe it comes from the 'poor me' role that children assume when they hear the word NO. When a child hears the word, *"NO,"* what does he do? He puts on a sad face and woefully looks at the NO-Sayer to get approval. He doesn't say, *"WOE is me!"* with words, but he says it with his expression. And guess what? It often works; he gets a hug and is forgiven. Now the child learns the false value of a woeful expression.

Many grownups have perfected the 'poor me' role. They simply repeat what they did as children, hoping it will give them the love and forgiveness they are looking for. Unfortunately, when a person makes 'poor me' his life's role, he grows bitter, feels cheated, and thinks that he's given so much, and for what? He feels that he's received so little in return.

Until a person is able to see himself as he really is, and comes to accept responsibility for what he has become, he will never be able to reach his full potential. How are you to play the role that you have always dreamed of playing, if you don't acknowledge that you have set NO-Traps for yourself and learn to recognize those traps so you can disable them? I will explain NO-Traps at a more appropriate time in the book.

WOE is everywhere

WOE is the ambient tone of our culture today. We watch woeful news reports on TV. We read of woeful financial conditions in the newspapers. We hear about woeful acts of crime on the radio, and our elected officials write more and more laws that say, "NO," hoping to avoid more WOE; some folks call it 'government control'.

The World Voice is a great barometer of how low our attitudes have sunk. When a culture operates from an attitude of WOE, everything bears that imprint. That common feeling of defeat leads to a collective feeling of depression, which is followed by an economic recession. Everyone assumes the cause is external, but, really, it's the prevailing attitude.

Human cultures are compilations of at-  titudes. When the collective attitude is depressed, the culture declines. If it's to get turned around, it requires one mind at a time. Each of us must learn what to obey and what to ignore. When we ignore WOE and obey our ambitious nature, eventually this new attitude collectively hits critical mass, and even the deepest recessions become upward expansions.

How do you help turn around a consciousness of scarcity and an attitude of WOE? Follow your naturally curious spirit. Make right corrections and you make the right connections. Soon, you find yourself surveying the world from a consciousness of prosperity. Magically, you add positive energy to the collective consciousness of humanity.

You know what I am saying is right. Knowing what's right is the first step to correcting what's wrong. You're an important force in this world. Act that way.

Cheap thrill

I remember when I'd get a cheap thrill from whining, "*WOE is me.*" I'd get some strange pleasure from feeling sorry for myself. I enjoyed believing I was right about all that was wrong with my life. This felt oddly reassuring, but it reinforced my 'poor me' identity.

We always derive some benefit from bad habits, however pointless the benefit may be. If we didn't think we would benefit, we would stop the behavior before it became a habit. It's a costly habit to wail out, "*WOE is me!*" in favor of so many other possible responses. This habit has you clinging to despair. When clinging to despair, you are clinging to a bear – it will rip you to shreds!

"*WOE has you clinging to despair.*
When clinging to despair,
you are clinging to a bear —
it will rip you to shreds!

Ask me today, "*What's wrong with life?*" and I'll respond, "*If something is wrong with my life, I am simply putting too much WOE into it.*" I prepared myself for thinking rightly by gathering right facts. This enabled me to proceed with my life logically, rather than in the illogical manner of my past.

Gigantic hoax

Hear this now: WOE is a gigantic hoax. WOE is a result of mental carelessness. WOE is the destructive use of the mind. Destructive use of the mind never offers constructive results. WOE serves no useful purpose. When you catch yourself saying, "*WOE is me,*" consider it an opportunity to correct. Drop the 'poor me' act.

Destructive use of the mind will never offer constructive results.

You reap what you sow. If you sow thoughts of NO, you reap a harvest of WOE. Don't let WOE rule your life and run it to ruin. Replace what's neurotic with what's healthy and natural. I've proven to myself, over and over again, that things never get worse when I let go of WOE – they only get better.

Ask yourself, *"Am I here to support an attitude of WOE?"* When you hear yourself saying No, now you are using the word NO correctly!

Let me offer you an escape plan from NO and WOE …

FOUR

The Great Escape

Prison bars

We experience deep feelings of resignation when our consciousness is saturated with NO and WOE. This feeling is revealing. It tells us that we've placed ourselves in psychological prison. The feeling of resignation feeds on echoes of NO and triggers memories of past failure and conjures up WOE.

WOE inhibits us from trying anything new. The harming effect of psychological prison is alarming. Psychological prison is a deplorable mental condition. It destroys our will to improve. This prison cell is filled with villainous mental voices that say misery and struggle are all we can expect.

Illuminating Tip: Howling NO's shackle the mind in chains, and the attitude of WOE places the mind behind bars.

Our feelings of inner imprisonment manifest themselves in myriad ways. You don't need to be a psychologist to know that we have a knack for acquiring bad habits that stop us from achieving our goals.

 Freedom of body is easy to recognize – one can go where one pleases. Freedom of mind, however, is a subtler matter. When one is mentally free, his attitude soars with visions of success, and he feels confident and eager to realize them. However, mental imprisonment is one of the greatest horrors of human living. We make choices and decisions that are never rewarding.

Hear the good news – you were born free, and you were born with talents and potential that can open a completely new world for you. Furthermore, you can be free again when you recognize that YOU placed yourself in mental prison. This happened when you put yourself in service to the regime of NO.

You, right now, have the power to escape the psychic captivity of WOE and experience sweet liberty. Escaping from psychological prison frees you of any recurring stress you experience in life. When stress free, you can see that you can be so much more than what you have been. This is a powerful new idea that can transform your life into an incredible adventure. Isn't that what life is really supposed to be about?

The feeling of personal freedom is the most enabling gift you can give yourself. Look within. See that part of you that wants to be free. Listen to it.

You are the jailer

Let's explore the matter of casting oneself into psychological prison a little further. You are both the jailer and the prisoner. No one has the power to place your naturally optimistic spirit behind bars except you. Others may lead you to the prison gate, but you have to walk through. No one has the key to set you free but you, and you have hidden the key. You hide the key when you listen to NO and wail out, "WOE!"

It's freeing when seeing the truth. Your mind has miraculous power to make your dreams come true. However, it must be free of NO and WOE if it's to perform its miracles. NO and WOE dull even the sharpest mind.

> *It's freeing when seeing the truth.*

When you shackle your mind in chains of NO and imprison your spirit with WOE, you feel it in your heart. You feel threatened by life. The threat is imaginary, but it feels damn real! Look into your own life to find where you have imprisoned your soaring spirit.

Student: *How can I determine whether I am in psychological prison or not?*

Teacher: *In what parts of your life do you feel intimidated? When do you feel inadequate or helpless? Is it with money matters? Relationships? Athletics? Education?*

Take ten minutes now to search through your life to see where you have imprisoned your soaring spirit by squelching your curious and ambitious nature. There was a time when I was afraid of money, and money was afraid of me. (It must have been afraid of me because it ran for cover whenever I tried to attract it to me.)

There is an unbreakable connection between the liberation of your curious mind and your ability to control your own destiny. Anything that takes away your inner freedom takes away your greatest treasure – your ability to make your mental abstractions real. What the mind can create in fantasy, the mind can create in reality, but this mind must be free.

Thinking back

Specifically, how do you place yourself in psychological prison? Perhaps showing you how I did it will help you understand how you do it. Thinking back, I can see that I did it in three steps:

STEP ONE: I'd begin with a positive affirmation: *"I'm going to start my own business, and make a million dollars in five years. Others do it; why not me?"*

Notice the question I'd tag onto the end of the positive affirmation. I would use this question to explain 'why NOT me'. I'd quickly move to:

STEP TWO: I'd say to myself, *"NO way! I'm not going to quit my job; I have too much time invested in it. Further, I don't want to lose my health benefits and retirement plan. That's why not me!"*

In this step, I used a NO to foster an attitude of WOE, thus placing myself in psychological prison. I could feel it; I was overcome with resignation. Now it was time to throw away the key, which was:

STEP THREE: I'd get angry; I'd look for examples of how I never got a break in my past, and I'd come up with reasons why I will never get a break now. This negative reaction locked in my woeful attitude and not only placed me in psychological prison, but guaranteed I'd serve more time there.

Of course, the healthy question to ask would have been: *"Is my anger due to a cruel world that is not cooperating with me, or is it due to my failure to see the truth?"* When I began asking myself this healthy question, I was able to see the futility of the strategy: Affirm a goal, howl, "NO," and wail, "WOE," until it creates inner oppression. I could see there was no intelligence to any of it. Inner oppression robs me of self-initiative, leaving me in psychological prison without a key. I now sigh quietly over such foolish behavior.

Are you ready to look at the strategy you've devised to place yourself in psychological prison? There's something that you'd love to be doing that would make you feel fully alive, but you're not doing it. What is it? What method do you use to avoid taking action? What do you say to yourself? How have you conditioned your mind to resist taking chances?

Ponder the above questions for ten minutes. Take notes on your thoughts. Learn the cause of your erroneous ways. If you can cause wrong in your life, you can cause right. Smile with delight, knowing that you are learning how to cause right.

Be honest with yourself, and take responsibility for being the jailer. With responsibility comes freedom. Freedom is a many-splendored thing!

Frederick Langbridge said, "Two men look out the same prison bars, one sees mud and the other stars." When looking down at the mud, we're caught in a pattern of thinking that causes painful deception. When looking up at the stars, we hear a faint inner whispering that offers right perception.

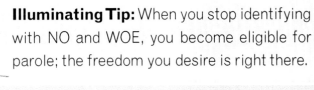

Illuminating Tip: When you stop identifying with NO and WOE, you become eligible for parole; the freedom you desire is right there.

NO-Test (NT)

It's time to take a NO-Test. You are at that place in the book where you're ready to do what NO's never want you to do. NO's prefer the darkness of your subconscious; it's time to expose these dark forces to the light. A great way to do this is to take a simple NO-Test. Your job is to be an objective observer and to take note of how harmful these forces can be.

Breathe away any tension that builds up while taking this NO-Test. Replace anxious thoughts by using the new knowledge you've acquired so far.

Grab a pen and paper, and prepare to write the truth. Go into a quiet room, no music, no visitors, no phone. If necessary, put a "DO NOT DISTURB!" sign on the door.

It is helpful to simply write the first thing that comes up while taking this test. Don't edit what you write. No one is going to read it but you.

Are you ready? Let's begin:

NT Question #1:

What do you do when a NO imposes on you? Do you have a cigarette, eat a Twinkie, make a drink, kick the dog, blame the world, or get mad at your mate?

Your answer: _____

Can you see how NO's compel you to do things that are against yourself rather than for yourself? NO's elicit your unconscious cooperation. It's time to stop cooperating.

NT Question #2:

How do NO's convince you to say, *"WOE!"?*
Be still. Allow the truth to come. If you listen
intently, you will hear the thought-voice that
accompanies NO. It will speak with its litany
of standard excuses: *"I don't have rhythm,
so I can't dance." "I'm big boned, so I can't
lose weight." "I'm not smart enough, so I
can't go to college." "I'm too old, so I can't
start my own business." "I'm too
young, so I can't start my own
business." "I'm bad at math, so
I can't balance my checkbook."*

Your answer: _____

Start writing, and don't stop until that
thought-voice stops. To understand the folly
of your excuses is to understand all you need
to know to withdraw your cooperation from
NO. The more confidently you separate excuse from fact, the quicker the NO's collapse.

> *The more confidently you separate excuse from fact, the quicker the NO's collapse.*

NT Question #3:

What do you *gain* by living with the consequences that come with your NO's? Do you get to be timid, lazy, angry, resentful? Do you get a headache and feel exhausted?

Your answer: _____

Can you see the insanity? You are unmasking the evil doings of NO. NO's promise that they will make you safe, but all they do is make you miserable.

You will never be free of NO until you willingly admit, *"I do this, all of this, to myself."* Foreign forces do not control your life; you cannot assume self command if you believe this superstition.

You win back your life by knowing what to obey and what not to obey. Here is a clue: Disobedience to NO is obedience to your ambitious and curious nature. Now it's up to you to choose wisely.

Don't argue to defend wrong tendencies and bad habits that you've uncovered with this NO-Test. Expose them to the light and recognize how they can overwhelm your will with impulsive urges that hamper your progress. Awareness guards against its happening in the future.

If you have excused yourself from taking the NO-Test, ask yourself, *"Is this my reaction to an old NO?"* One admission like this can break a pattern that has been going on for years.

Something noble and beautiful is happening to you. You are learning to withhold power from the forces that have lured you into playing the role of victim. You are a victim only when you do not see what is happening. You are opening your eyes to the truth and soon you will see that you've always held the key to sweet liberty.

Rumbling thunder is harmless

When I was small, I'd hide in my closet during a thunderstorm. I was afraid of thunder. Its rumbling noise scared me. One day, mom came in and sat with me. She told me that thunder is harmless. She explained how driving rain can cause leaks in the roof,  and strong winds can topple over the lawn chairs, and lightning can cause a fire in the backyard. *"BUT,"* she emphasized, *"The rumbling thunder cannot harm you."*

Mom's good, protective voice convinced me that I was safe no matter how loud the thunder rumbled. In that moment, I was no longer the naïve child when it came to rumbling thunder.

It's time now to face the truth about your inner storms rumbling with NO. Listen to that good, protective voice deep within you. It is telling you that rumbling cannot harm you. Your fearful reactions can cause a woeful condition, but the rumbling of NO is harmless.

> *Howling NO's are as harmless as the rumbling of thunder in a thunderstorm.*

Affirming and visualizing is not enough

When I deluded myself into believing the rumble of a thunderstorm could harm me, I suffered woefully. There are many ways that we delude ourselves and suffer woefully. I remember several times when I affirmed an aspiration and visualized an outcome but refused to deal with past NO's. I'd read a book that said that affirming and visualizing was all that it took to succeed. I'd been deluded into believing this, and the consequences were woeful. This common misconception has caused many folks grief.

It's popular today to say that the Law of Attraction will accommodate you if you take the time to visualize your dreams. Thinking this is all there is to succeeding is the beginning of delusion.

Indeed, visualizing an outcome that you desire to achieve, while feeling optimistic and confident, will surely attract ways and means of realizing your

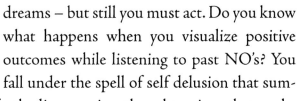

dreams – but still you must act. Do you know what happens when you visualize positive outcomes while listening to past NO's? You fall under the spell of self delusion that summons forth discouraging thought-voices that make you hesitate and procrastinate. Therefore, even if the ways and means of realizing your dreams were available, you'd debate their validity.

Seek the truth; it brings clarity to confusion, which ends delusion. When delusion ends, healing begins. Earnestly seeking the truth requires letting go of old patterns of thought that stop your naturally curious and ambitious spirit from working in your favor.

You will never realize your creative power as long as you operate under the delusion that affirming your dreams without dealing with old NO's is sufficient. The mind is dazed by this delusion, and its reasoning faculties are compromised.

To end any delusion, you must first recognize it and acknowledge the harm it is doing. I'd still be hiding in my room during thunderstorms if my mother had not shown me that I'd deluded myself into believing something that isn't true.

The only reason anyone falls short of achieving his dreams is because he has deluded himself into believing he is in some essential way, inadequate (which comes from listening to old NO's). What does this person inevitably do? He proves to himself that his false belief is true by subconsciously sabotaging any attempts he makes to succeed.

A symptom of suffering under the fundamental delusion of being inadequate is the compulsion to prove the validity of this false proposition. I call this the NO-Delusion. It is characterized by the lament, *"I just don't have what it takes to be a winner."* When this is spoken with conviction, one gets involved in trivial and useless matters that drain all his strength.

A symptom of a NO-Delusion is the inability to see opportunities as anything other than obstacles. Can you recall an opportunity that you missed because you couldn't see the possibility of succeeding because you were focusing on the probability of failing?

The feeling that is often associated with a NO-Delusion is the feeling of being cheated. The healthy response is to accept that you're exactly where you chose to be because you succumbed to this negative condition. Accepting this fact enables you to break free of the self-enslavement that comes with being deluded by NO.

A mind deluded by NO is a fearful, hampered mind. It has forgotten its power; it must be reminded. If you poisoned your body, you would take any measure to rid your body of the poison. Let it be the same with your mind.

> *A mind that has forgotten its power, must be reminded.*

Your mind is your playground

Make your mind your playground. It's a beautiful thing. Use it this way. Consider NO's as evil visitors who turn your playground into a place of torment. The word 'evil' is the word 'live' spelled backwards. To *live* is to spring forward, to soar upward with a consciousness of abundance and prosperity. When under the NO-Delusion, you fall backward; you spiral downward with a consciousness of lack and deprivation – that's just *evil*.

When you hear NO's howling on your playground, don't howl back. South American Howler monkeys do that. Don't join that pack. See joining that pack as a wrong act. When you take control, you end the ache of WOE that accompanies an evil NO.

> *When you take control, you end the ache of WOE that accompanies an evil NO.*

A great way to take control, and close your mental playground to howling NO's, is to say, "*Foul play!*" Say it with the authority of a referee. You're doing what NO's hate – you're calling them on their cunning game of deceit. "*Foul play!*" is a fabulous NO-Stopper. This is an empowering fact. Never hesitate to act on an empowering fact.

The tormenting poke of NO is just a poor joke. The next time you hear yourself lamenting, "*WOE,*" you'll know you've been poked. Now you know what to say – "*Foul play!*" This will give you the moment you need to pause, take a breath, and recognize the delusional nature of this feeling of inadequacy. It gives you strength to act in your own best interest. Just know-ing that you can take action is invigorating .

Illuminating Tip: Weakness is ignorance of NO; strength is awareness of NO, and taking the time to call, *"Foul play!"*

The NO-Free Zone

You escape to the NO-Free Zone when you banish NO from making decisions in your life. The NO-

Free Zone is a delightful state of con-sciousness where you no longer listen to inner voices that sneer at everything good and beautiful about you.

When you look at yourself from the NO-Free Zone, you're in tune with the whole of your unlimited po-tential. This puts you in flow, which further opens your mind to all that it needs to know to banish NO as a decision maker.

NO cannot harm your health or ruin your relation-ships without your permission. It may still try to flood your mind with useless opinions, but when you're in the NO-Free Zone, you don't listen. You find yourself laughing, wondering how you could have ever surrendered so much control to NO. Now, you are free to address your life without distraction; hence, you're WOE free.

> **Student:** *Is there a limit to what you can do in the NO-Free Zone?*

> **Teacher:** *No one has reached that limit yet.*

The NO-Free Zone is a place of relaxed silence where you are:

- *Passively watchful*

- *Serenely ready*

- *Calmly focused*

This non-hostile state of mind is incredibly powerful. Have you ever been passively watchful as someone acted out his drama about some matter in his life? You, emotionally detached, can plainly see the issues and solutions, but he, emotionally charged, is blind to them. When NO-Free, you are able to do this with your own life.

Hearing an old NO in a state of relaxed silence is an utterly different experience from hearing it in a state of emotional turmoil. Relaxed and quiet, you simply put that old NO in its place, back in the past, where it belongs.

When I first learned about affirming my goals, I did not know what I now know, and I'd recite my affirmations with aggressive silence; I'd shout inwardly, "*I can do this if I set my mind to it!*" Aggressive silence is a form of mental violence that reinforces old NO's. This is why it is important to learn to practice calm focus when affirming your goals. Calm focus places your mind in the NO-Free Zone. When NO-Free, there are no feelings of inadequacy, and you act in ways that effect the changes you desire.

> *Aggressive silence is a form of mental violence that reinforces old NO's.*

This book is showing you many ways to achieve calm focus. Here are some NO-Free Zone rules to further help you with this.

Rules of the NO-Free Zone:

Rule #1: No pushing.

NO's are hostile and pushy, but don't you push back.

Don't argue. Don't disagree.

Resistance encourages persistence.

The NO's you resist today, will just come back tomorrow.

Pushing prompts NO-Attacks.

Pushing at an old NO is like throwing a ball against a wall – the more force you put into throwing the ball, the more force the ball has to bounce back. NO's react like that!

Rule #2: Don't suppress.

Suppression doesn't solve problems; it causes problems.

When you hear a NO howling, don't try to suppress it by getting mad about something else.

Madness invites badness into your life.

So, what should you do? If you've been paying attention, you know what to do: Unmask the falsehood of NO by bringing it into the light of truth.

RULE #3: Don't join the flock of cawing crows.

William Blake said, "*The eagle never lost so much time as when he submitted to learn of the crow.*" Cawing crows are those who gather to lament, "*Oh NO! ... WOE, WOE, WOE!*" They are fiercely eager to affirm the dismal proposition that life doesn't work.

Don't go along with NO-Sayers just to get along with them.

If you're to walk into the NO-Free Zone, you must quietly walk away from folks who are cawing.

Rule #4: Don't deny that NO's exist.

Be honest.

Commit to a thorough assessment of the damage that NO's have done to you in wasted energy and squandered time.

Delay no longer – delaying is the worst kind of denial.

Stand in wise silence.

"To be wiser than other men is to be honester than they; and strength of mind is only courage to see and speak the truth." - William Hazlitt

Do you like that? Then do that.

An escape plan is now in your hands

You now have an escape plan in your hands. Progress quickens when you obey the rule of "First Things First." When you learn how to avoid the first error, which is listening to old NO's, it's easy to avoid the second error, which is to lament, *"WOE!"*

You are motivated to stop listening to NO once you recognize it for what it is – an imposter, pretending to have your best interests at heart while secretly laughing with contempt as it works to destroy your dreams.

Open one small portal to the truth, and the needed light will shine to reveal other important truths. NO's tremble in the face of truth; the disruptive force of NO ends when you realize that the source of all its power is faulty thinking, which is coming from your own mistaken mind.

You now know how to use your mind to rid your mind of mistaken beliefs. This knowledge alters your course. You have already shaken the foundation of your *woe is me* identity. Can you feel the difference?

Stop and think. What do you imagine happens when you bring your mind back to its naturally ambitious and curious nature? It's time to introduce you to the power of WOW....

FIVE

The Power of WOW

The dynamic of words

The English essayist, Aldous Huxley, theorized that, when learning a language, we inherit the wisdom of those who spoke the language before us. He said the words carry the wisdom. I agree. I also believe that we inherit the madness of humanity when we hear the word NO, 60,000 times. This single word has negatively impacted generations of human beings in myriad ways, especially when spoken with an authoritative voice that demands strict submission.

Perhaps it's impossible to stop the world at large from overusing the word NO, but you can limit your own use. Moreover, when you control the impulse to say, "NO," the urge to say, "WOE" falls away. NO and WOE are anxiety-provoking twins. You lift yourself above the effect of these twin words when you work on withdrawing NO from your vocabulary.

Unlocking your potential with a simple word

In the absence of using the word NO, you'll have room for all kinds of brilliant alternatives. My personal favorite is the word, WOW. You will be amazed at how easily WOW can replace NO and WOE. Furthermore WOW is a confidence builder, it's an expression of wonder.

The word WOW opens your mind to endless possibilities. When you say *WOW* with enthusiasm, it elevates your disposition to a soaring *YES-to-life*. It boosts your spirit so you can rise above adversity with curiosity and self command.

WOW is my acronym for:

Wonderfully Obsessed *with* Winning.

When **WOW** becomes an attitude, one is **W**onderfully **O**bsessed with **W**inning at the game of life. He eagerly prepares for higher levels of achievement by finding every possible YES in every situation. He gets great satisfaction out of exploring his enormous potential.

Can you see how you've wasted yourself on the words NO and WOE? WOW offers a very different perspective from the downwardly spiraling attitude that comes with NO and WOE. It gives you a fresh look at life. I am basing this claim on how my own attitude changed when I replaced WOE with WOW.

Your attitude has everything to do with your successes and failures in life, and your words have everything to do with your attitude. Say, "WOW," to what you're reading right now. You receive great truths to the degree that you value them, so say, "WOW," to remind you to value what you're learning.

There was a time when I feared the flu. As soon as the cold winter came, I'd begin wailing, "*WOE, the flu season is upon us.*" I succeeded at getting the flu annually for years until I read an article on the immense power of the immune system. I found myself saying, "*WOW, I had no idea.*" I valued what I'd learned, my attitude changed about getting the flu, and I've not had the flu since.

Speaking beyond NO and WOE

When I made a conscious decision to speak beyond NO and WOE, I slowly but increasingly began trusting myself in ways that I never did before. I developed the resolve to make small but progressive steps toward  my goals. I improved the quality of my responses to challenging matters in my life. I noticed when I was doing unnecessary things and I'd make corrections, quickly.

You succeed at what you did, repeatedly, yesterday, and you will succeed at what you do, repeatedly, today. When you make it a habit to transform the attitude of WOE to WOW, and attempt to achieve something fresh and new today, you soon find yourself acting in ways that give you optimal results tomorrow.

If you give it some thought, I imagine you can attest to having had WOW experiences from time to time, in your own life. It's valuable to observe what offers you inspiring feelings of inner newness so it doesn't seem so mysterious and difficult to repeat.

Words guide us through life. WOW lifts us up and WOE drags us down. WOW heals and WOE wounds. The word WOW is a maker of triumphant successes, and the word NO is a sure success breaker. Emerson said, "The world makes way for a man who knows where he is going." The man who is **W**onderfully **O**bsessed with **W**inning is the man who knows where he is going; he refuses to be discouraged by adversity.

It is correct to say that the source of your success is always inside of you. It's never the world that creates your successes and failures, but rather, it's the words you use within yourself, while looking at the world, that determine whether you will succeed or fail.

Student: *What makes it so difficult to refrain from using NO and WOE?*

Teacher: *It's a thought-habit that requires self-discipline and patience to overcome.*

Your inward self-talk seems to ramble on its own, but the truth is that these thought-voices have no power to speak beyond what you have repeatedly thought. They simply parrot these thoughts back to you. You can rein in your self-talk by adding a simple word like WOW to your vocabulary, and using it daily.

Study yourself as you make an effort to make WOW a part of your inward self-talk. Notice how this word elevates your attitude. Notice how this elevated attitude takes over your self-talk and inspires you to shout, "YES," to life.

Illuminating Tip: WOW supports one's intuitive intelligence and naturally soaring spirit.

WOW makes self-help books valuable

Before discovering the power of WOW, I'd read hundreds of self-help books. I thought these books would change me as an individual. I thought they would inspire me to do great things. Yet nothing changed. Were the books making false promises? The problem was not with the books; the problem was with me, with my attitude.

I'd read the books with an attitude of WOE and, even though I could see the logic in what the books offered, I didn't really believe it would work for me. The belief was subconscious, but clearly it was there. This one belief rendered the books useless to me.

When I began holding myself responsible for the words I used with my inward self-talk, I returned to some of my favorite self-help books with a new attitude, an attitude of WOW, and was amazed at how stubborn I'd been. I actually began applying the tips to my life. "The realization of truth is brought about by perception, and not in the least by ten millions of acts." - Adi Shankara.

WOW supports a consciousness of success, which inspires millions of small acts that place a person in the winner's circle of life. However, without a consciousness of success, the acts are ineffective. There is a direct connection between the soaring spirit that follows WOW and one's level of achievement.

A mind possessed with a consciousness of success is uninhibited, eager and efficient. Nothing is as powerful as a mind that believes in its capacity to win. A person with such a mind achieves things that seem absolutely impossible to the woeful onlooker.

> *A mind possessed with a consciousness of success is uninhibited, eager and efficient.*

I believe WOW is instinctive. Small children intuitively feel it, and they love saying, "*WOW!*" It's what motivates them to begin speaking by age one and understanding most of what is said to them by age three.

It's a healthy act to transfer one's allegiance from WOE back to WOW. When you let WOE go, you disengage from life's melodrama. Your energy is now available for setting a course of action that adds greater depth to your existence. It's never too late to create a *WOWsome* life.

Inspiring Addiction

Do you know what happens when you're gripped by an attitude of WOW? You transform your hopes and dreams into *inspiring addictions*. Now you have a mighty dynamo working for you – a *wonderful obsession* to achieve your aspiration and an *inspiring addiction*, an invigorating craving that gives you staying power even in the face of great odds.

It's an incredible feeling to be motivated by an invigorating craving when setting one's sights on a goal. It compels advantageous action, even under the most disadvantageous conditions.

We usually consider an addiction a harmful habit of action, but what if the habit of action lifts your attitude so you learn from your action? What if the habit sharpens your sensitivity to life's countless combinations of opportunities? What if it motivates you to express yourself in a positive fashion, with no inhibitions? This is what happens when you are *inspiringly addicted*. Is this harmful?

Helen Keller was deaf and blind. She developed an *inspiring addiction* to break through the isolation of her afflictions. This addiction motivated her to accomplish extraordinary things. She became a world famous speaker and author.

Martin Luther King, Jr., developed an *inspiring addiction* to assist all members of the human race, so they could access their unrealized potential. He understood his value in the world when he developed an *inspiring addiction* to help improve the world.

Imagine being *inspiringly addicted* to a cause that would make a positive difference in the world. When you are *inspiringly addicted*, you give yourself more earnestly to reflection and come to understand your value in the world. What do you suppose would satisfy your soul more than that?

Inspiring addictions wipe out old mental pictures of disappointing failure, which leaves you with a clean mental screen on which to project bright new scenes. Imagine feeling invigoratingly compelled to set goals that make your life meaningful. Imagine feeling *inspiringly addicted* to solving new problems that teach you how to handle difficulty with poise.

Indeed, *wonderful obsessions* and *inspiring addictions* are a powerful duo – they bring out the best in you. Moreover, when you accept this reality you experience yourself as a super self-sufficient being, which is what you truly are. Are you ready to give up the easy but unhealthy comfort you get from WOE? Are you ready to reach for WOW?

Wonderful obsessions and inspiring addictions are a powerful duo.

WOW is not problem free

WOW stands behind everything great that has ever been achieved. WOW stands behind everything great that you have ever achieved. However, don't misunderstand me; an attitude of WOW is not problem

free. When your attitude is soaring, you take greater risks, and with greater risks come greater problems. However, when you're wonderfully obsessed with solving the problems, you gain insights that help you find solutions that bring new meaning to your life.

> *WOW stands behind everything great that has ever been achieved.*

WOW may not be problem free, but it takes you out of servitude to NO and into the freedom of self command. Imagine being **W**onderfully **O**bsessed with **W**inning in all domains of living: mental, physical, spiritual, emotional, financial, social, and with family. There is no better way to improve your quality of life than to continually study the ways of your mind. The benefits are unlimited when you understand how your mind works. With this knowledge you can transform it into a compelling force for good. Soon, you find every day feels like a supremely successful day.

There is no better way to improve your quality of life than to continually study the ways of your mind.

Give it up

Have you ever noticed that you often have to give up something in order to get something new? To become a different kind of person, I had to give up the foolish pleasure I got from lamenting, "WOE is me," when things weren't working out. I also had to give up my membership to the 'Cawing Crows Club' by no longer gathering with naysayers who insisted they were right about how wrong life is.

When I understood how petty my woeful attitude was, and was willing to give it up, I was delighted with what came naturally to me – the attitude of WOW. Clinging to my woeful attitude never relieved my feelings of inadequacy and insecurity. Can you see the insanity?

I imagine you've observed how children love saying WOW. Now you can see how unfortunate it is that they eventually learn to imitate their parents' expressions of WOE. Are you still imitating expressions of WOE that you learned years ago? It's time to give it up; it's time get back to the richness of your natural attitude.

"Tomorrow, and tomorrow, and tomorrow, creeps in this petty pace from day to day, to the last syllable of recorded time ... Life's but a walking shadow, a poor player that struts and frets his hour upon the stage, and then is heard no more. It is a tale told by an idiot, full of sound and fury, signifying nothing." – William Shakespeare. These are the tomorrows that WOE offers.

Finding right answers and making right choices requires a WOE-Free mind. WOW is always the right way to go. How easily we are led astray by our own illogical thinking. Stop insisting that NO and WOE is the way to go, and your tomorrows will take on a new glow.

Get excited right now about giving up your excuses for lamenting WOE, no matter how valid it feels. Right there, you will find an exhilarating WOW waiting.

The importance of opposites

You might be asking, "Why does WOE have to exist at all?" Well, unfortunately, in this world of polarity, there cannot be a North Pole if its polar opposite, the South Pole, doesn't exist. How can there be an East Coast without a West Coast? If everyone was tall, and no one was small, could there be an experience of tall? This same logic applies to WOW and WOE. How are you to experience the high of a wonderful obsession, if you've never felt the low of woeful whining?

The Chinese philosopher Lao Tsu, said, "*Under heaven all can see beauty only as beauty, only because there is ugliness. Therefore having and not having arise together. Difficult and easy complement each other.*" You can see WOW as beautiful, only because you have seen the ugliness of WOE. Therefore WOW and WOE arise together, they actually complement each other, but which will shape your attitude is entirely up to you.

By the choices you make, you determine which is to dominate and which is to submit – WOW or WOE. Here's a three-step process that forces WOE to submit:

STEP 1: Look at some recurring problem in your life and say, *"WOW ... this exists only with my cooperation."* You must accept responsibility for the problem if you are to have the power to rid yourself of it.

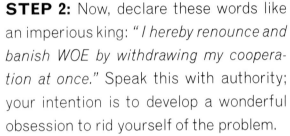

STEP 2: Now, declare these words like an imperious king: *" I hereby renounce and banish WOE by withdrawing my cooperation at once."* Speak this with authority; your intention is to develop a wonderful obsession to rid yourself of the problem.

STEP 3: Now chant in a joyous tone, *"If it is to be, it is up to me."* Soon you will realize that WOW does not come from some mysterious or remote source in the heavens; it comes directly from you.

Never underestimate your own power. Never underestimate the power of WOW, which is your own power. Furthermore, you have the ability to create *WOW at will* – it's your prerogative to transform your emotions into a compelling force for good. This power deserves respect.

"You can create WOW at will.

Take a moment to reflect on this prerogative. You are a member of a race (the human race) whose members have the divine right to take command of their minds and create an attitude of *WOW at will*, which renders WOE helpless. It's time to base your everyday decisions on this knowledge. This is never a mistake to do. It's fun doing positive things for yourself, isn't it.

What's worthy of your WOW?

What's worthy of your WOW? What's a commendable reason for being obsessed? What vision of success is worthy of your passion? What aspiration do you value enough to convert into an inspiring addiction?

By taking time to answer questions like the above, you train your mind to think constructively. And if while asking such questions you hear a sneering voice, recognize it for what it is – an old NO. Let it go.

It's natural to crave good things. Intense desire makes your dreams important and durable, which makes it easier to lay your defeats behind you. What you lay behind you will stay behind you when you are **W**onderfully **O**bsessed with **W**inning in life.

I personally love the refreshment that WOW provides. It invigorates my spirit by reminding me that there is plenty of time and plenty of world available to make my life an ongoing adventure. What do you suppose could be worthier than that?

People who live successful, happy lives have the same creative power that you have; they are not endowed with any special power that's unavailable to you. They simply deny old NO's so the pervasive power of WOW can take control, and they decide what goals are worthy of WOW.

Everyone carries greatness within; it's the power of WOW that releases it. WOW revives the YES-Habit when you contemplate visions of success. You were born with the YES-Habit; it's time to revive it. Never sacrifice an opportunity to grow in order to please an old NO. This one piece of advice can bring sweet release from WOE, thus helping you develop the YES-Habit.

> *Never sacrifice an opportunity to grow in order to please an old NO.*

Choose what's worthy of WOW right now, by asking yourself:

"How can I use WOW in my life right now?"
"How can I use WOW in my life right now?"
"How can I use WOW in my life right now?"

I don't know when you're going to take this question seriously, maybe tomorrow, maybe the next day, maybe right now. The intelligent person recognizes the worthiness of using WOW wisely. With right effort, you will understand the importance of this truth. You'll notice internal changes occurring when you do.

Joyful success comes from WOW

Joyful success comes from WOW. Joyful success does not come from putting your nose to the grindstone and unduly struggling, trying to pay your dues in service to old NO's. This approach to succeeding in life can only support an attitude of WOE, which thwarts your best intentions every time.

Think back to a time when things went incredibly well, when you joyfully succeeded at something new. Do you remember that wonderful state of mind? Was getting what you wanted really a matter of putting your nose to the grindstone and unduly struggling? More and more, you are discovering what's been wrong with your attitude so you can make it right.

Ambrose Redmoon advised: "Courage is not the absence of fear but rather the judgment that something else is more important than the fear." When you assign WOW a worthy cause, you make the judgment that joyful success is more important than fear. Now you find all the courage you need to face any adversity that tries to stop you from succeeding.

Fear, in most circumstances, is nothing more than the woeful experience one gets when listening to old NO's. Hear this marvelous message: Choose WOW, and you will have the courage to be a new and happy person who chooses joyful success repeatedly.

When looking at the future, you have one of two fundamental choices to make: *Look and Know* … or …

NO-Go. When you *Look and Know,* you imagine a future filled with joyful successes and know it shall be so. That's because you have the courage to do whatever it takes to make it so. When you choose *NO-Go,* you consider a future of joyful success as nothing more than foolish fantasy, and you say, "NO," when it's time to go forward.

> *When looking at the future, you have one of two fundamental choices to make:* Look and Know ... or ... NO-Go.

WOW supplies psychological refreshment

An attitude of WOW supplies psychological refreshment that always boosts your spirit. This is what makes it so practical. If it isn't practical, it isn't spiritual, and you're on a spiritual journey right now. If you're paying attention to what you're reading right now, then it's dawning on you that you're beginning to look at your life from a very different perspective than usual.

Ask yourself again, *"How can I use WOW in my life right now?"* How can you use WOW to look at negative circumstances differently – right now? How can you put WOW to work in your daily affairs - right now? How can you use WOW to think constructively about that work project – right now? Allow the feeling of renewed power to rise up within you. Savor the psychological refreshment it offers.

WOW is the most powerful of positive forces; it's the stuff of which faith is made; it's a spiritual experience. You purify your action when you put WOW into it.

It's important to know what to value. You suffer when you value wrong things. Let's look at a few reasons for valuing WOW over WOE:

When you value WOW, you value winning.
When you value WOE, you value whining.

KA-CHING: Score 1 for **WOW**.

When you value WOW, you value solutions.
When you value WOE, you value drama.

KA-CHING: Score 2 for **WOW**.

When you value WOW, you value freedom.
When you value WOE, you value
servitude to NO.

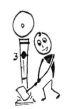

KA-CHING: Score 3 for **WOW**.

When you value WOW, you value
feeling *self-sufficient*.
When you value WOE, you value
feeling *self-deficient*.

KA-CHING: Score 4 for **WOW**.

When you value WOW, you value your
inspiring daydreams.
When you value WOE, you value
your nightmares.

KA-CHING: Score 5 for **WOW**.

GAME OVER!

A glance at the above score sheet shows the importance of disobeying any impulse you have to wail out, "WOE." Albert Einstein defined insanity as doing the same thing repeatedly, and expecting different results. This gets right to the point. When you wail out, "WOE," repeatedly, and expect a different result, you've *temporarily misplaced your sanity.* If this is making sense to you, then you've made a fabulous start in the right direction.

Using Humor

I like the phrase, *"I've temporarily misplaced my sanity."* I use it when I catch myself reacting to echoes of old NO's. The phrase brings humor to the moment. Humor is a powerful resource that places us 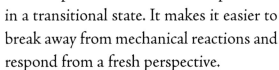 in a transitional state. It makes it easier to break away from mechanical reactions and respond from a fresh perspective.

James Long said, "One reason God created time was so that there would be a place to bury the failures of the past." Failures of the past often carry NO's with them; therefore, it's important to leave failures of the past in the past, where they belong.

One of the great skills of the mind is its ability to travel backwards in time. Nothing else does this. Neither light nor time travels backwards. The planet does not reverse its rotation. So, what's the reason the mind can float back in time? It is for learning purposes. If we're looking at old mental movies of past failures, hoping to change things back there, then we've temporarily misplaced our sanity, haven't we?

Having knowledge of what went wrong can be powerful if we use it to make things right, but to dwell in the knowledge and feel miserable about it is insane. Here's a way that I bring lightheartedness to moments when I find my mind drifting back in time and dwelling on past failures.

I imagine walking by a hospital where an ambulance siren is blaring.

I ask the medic who's rushing to the ambulance, *"What's happening?"*

He shouts, *"I'm responding to an accident that happened thirty years ago."*

I say, *"That's crazy! Have you temporarily misplaced your sanity?"*

I then say to myself, *"Like the medic, I've temporarily misplaced my sanity when I react to howling sirens of NO from failures of thirty years ago."*

I find this scene helps break the chain of time that binds me to old NO's. Do you like this strategy? Then use this strategy.

Psychological crimes

I consider it a *psychological crime* when I use my mind in an unreasonable way. The English poet Walter Savage Landor said, "We oftener say things because we can say them well, than because they are sound and reasonable." I oftener said, "WOE," because I could say it well, not because it was sound and reasonable.

Now, when I catch myself saying WOE, or anything of the sort, I pause to declare it a *psychological crime*. I imagine pinning a sheriff's badge on my chest and declaring myself the enforcer of the law in my exclusive territory – my field of consciousness. The badge has a big WOW stamped on it.

As I pin the badge on my chest, I say, "*When it comes to my field of consciousness, I am the law. I will not allow childhood echoes of NO to invade my territory. I declare it a* psychological crime *to participate in woeful thinking. It is against the laws of my original nature to speak in terms of WOE, and I won't tolerate it.*" This humorous statement is a wonderful pattern interrupter. It gives me breathing room to shift my perspective.

Become suspicious whenever you feel a WOE invading your exclusive territory. Pause and grant yourself authority to rid your conditioned mind of negative programming. Declare yourself the sheriff. The more you understand the mechanics of your mind, the easier it is to take command. Understanding is a powerful resource that helps you make corrections.

Use your new awareness of unwanted mental conditions as a motivating force. Do whatever it takes to replace WOE with a good laugh. The rewards are incredible. WOW will show up. WOW is a many-splendored thing!

Two Minds

I find it easier to understand the mind when I consider that I have two of them. I was born with a *freethinking mind* and by age six I developed a second mind, a *conditioned mind*.

The *freethinking mind* does not look to conditioned memories to come up with answers; it's an open mind that supports my free will. That's an extraordinary thing, right there.

My *conditioned mind* only thinks as it has been trained to think. It operates in service to old patterns of thought that are etched on my brain and stored in the subconscious. The *conditioned mind* demands that I react mechanically to circumstances, like one of Pavlov's dogs. Pavlov's dogs were conditioned to salivate when a bell rang. The conditioned mind wants me to wail out WOE when a NO howls.

This *conditioned mind* is an unfaithful servant because it is loyal to the old NO's. It is stubbornly impertinent when I try something new.

Great philosophers and great thinkers, through the ages, speak of the richness we lose when we give up our *freethinking mind*. If you're skeptical about what you're reading right now, ask yourself which mind is in control, right now – the *freethinking* or the *conditioned* mind.

Now comes a happy fact: you can use your *freethinking mind* to declare independence from the *conditioned mind*. You can use your *freethinking mind* to detach from your compulsive need to react to howling NO's. Happy days! Doing this is beneficial in all ways – you experience better health, you develop an alluring personality, and you are more productively active.

In the past, I would take it personally when someone differed with me. One day, a friend urged me to notice how this pattern controlled me. He asked, *"How are you going to grow if your conditioned mind always screams, "NO," to anything new?* In that moment, a memory came to me. I was in a third grade spelling bee and I misspelled the word *ghost*. The teacher said,

 *"NO, that's wrong ... sit down Bobby."* Two of my friends tormented me all the way home from school by mimicking the teacher and repeatedly saying, *"NO, that's wrong ... sit down Bobby!"*

I've learned that I'm not here to serve the conditioned mind that was programmed back in the third grade. I no longer react like a puppet on a string when someone suggests that I'm wrong about something. I remind myself that the third grade experience is just an old mental movie, and it cannot affect my mood today unless I foolishly turn it on and watch it.

Murphy's Law vs. WOW

I find that whenever I succumb to WOE, I invoke Murphy's Law. Murphy's Law says: *If anything can go wrong, it will.* How astonishing that we have a law to explain what happens when we let WOE dominate our attitude.

Johann Wolfgang von Goethe said, *"Until one is committed, there is hesitancy, the chance to draw back, always ineffectiveness."* I believe that hesitating, drawing back, and ineffective action is a consequence of woeful thinking, which invokes Murphy's Law. Certainly, with that kind of behavior, if anything can go wrong, it will. How is one to commit to anything new while thinking from a conditioned mind that says, *"NO, NO, NO"!*

Later in the same quote, Goethe says that when we are willing to commit, *"All sorts of things occur to help one that would never otherwise have occurred."* WOW, what a curious and healthy piece of knowledge this is. So, Murphy's Law has a counterpart! Goethe calls this counterpart – *providence*. He says that *providence* helps the person who's committed. What better way to commit than to begin with an attitude of WOW?

The *freethinking mind* encourages you to call on WOW so you may dance freely like nobody's watching. The *conditioned mind* encourages you to call on WOE, and then dance like a lifeless puppet, connected to a string of old NO's. When you dance with life freely, providence moves to help you. When you dance like a puppet, you invoke Murphy's Law. Which will it be?

YES-Shouts have no clout

YES-Shouts have no clout when shouted from an attitude of WOE. I imagine you understand this by now. An attitude of WOE flips the YES/NO switch in your mind to NO. When the switch is flipped to NO, it matters not how loud you shout, "YES!"

> *YES-Shouts have no clout when shouted from an attitude of WOE.*

When you simply shout, "YES!" to rid yourself of a howling NO, you place yourself on a psychological seesaw: shout "YES," and feel high … hear a howling NO, and feel low; shout, "YES," feel high again … hear a howling NO, again you feel low. The attachment to NO puts you in a psychologically fixed position that pulls you back down, no matter how loud you shout, "YES," to feel up.

Thinking a YES-Shout will help you achieve your goals, while caught in an attitude of WOE, drags you further into the morass. The old proverb, "If wishes were horses, beggars would ride," is as valid today as it was four hundred years ago.

Plato declared, "There is nothing so delightful as the hearing or speaking of truth." The truth is that you cannot ignore the villainous voice of NO by merely shouting, "YES!" There is another part to this truth, which is absolutely empowering: *As certain as YES-Shouts have no clout when bellowed from an attitude of WOE, a quiet 'yes' contains no doubt when whispered from an attitude of WOW!*

YES is your inherent right, and this is because WOW is your natural inclination. An attitude of WOW flips the YES/NO switch to YES. Trust what you are hearing right now. With a flexible mind and a firm will to prove that YES is your inherent right, you will discover healthy ways of turning a lethargic YES into a dynamic YES.

Henry David Thoreau said, "If men would steadily observe realities only, and not allow themselves to be deluded, life, to compare it with such things as we know, would be like a fairy tale …" You, too, can know what Thoreau knew. However, you must be willing to question every limiting belief that you now hold as precious and true. Imagine no longer allowing old NO's to delude you – what fairy tale might unfold for you?

Be inconsiderate

Happiness and success come to those who are inconsiderate of WOE. When hearing a WOE, know that your life is out of control. It's time to deliberately interrupt the inward self-talk. Here's another statement I like to make: *"I'm not falling for your trickery. You offer no value, why would I listen to you?"* When I say this and mean it, I have the power to cancel dozens of WOEs immediately.

Happiness and success come to those who are inconsiderate of WOE.

The best way to be inconsiderate of WOE is to be considerate of WOW. WOW needs a focus if it's to work effectively for you. It needs something solid to act on. When you focus your WOW on a worthy objective, you're being considerate of it. You're also being rude to NO.

It's in your best interest to be rude to any inward self-talk that keeps you from thinking clearly and intelligently. A focused WOE brings out the worst in you. A focused WOW brings out the best in you. A mind that conceives great things with an attitude of WOW, can achieve great things.

Man's greatest achievements begin as daydreams backed by a focused WOW. Focusing WOW on a mental abstraction is essential to putting it into action. One of your greatest gifts is the ability to give direction to the sustaining force of WOW. When you gather the energy this force offers, and point it to where you want to go, it's called purposeful living. Now that's a noble aim!

When one lives with purpose, he is incredibly resourceful; he finds ways and means of accomplishing the most challenging tasks. Observe a great athlete, musician, scientist, or anyone who's living purposefully; notice how he takes full advantage of the powers of his mind. His natural powers seem to take on supernatural qualities.

> **Illuminating Tip:** Small minds submit to the control of WOE; great minds control life with the power of WOW.

What personal dare have you conquered with a focused WOW? It was a lot of fun, wasn't it. The force of focused energy is inspiring. When you concentrate your WOW energy, it shows in everything you do. It rouses your mind to find new ideas in old facts and it motivates you to act on those new ideas.

Share the WOW's

Your first calling is always to help yourself. Moreover, a great way to help yourself is to do what's valuable for you – do what it takes to get your daily dose of WOW. When you succeed with this, what naturally follows is your second calling – to help others. And the best way to do this is by helping others experience WOW.

 The Golden rule says that we should do to others what we'd like them to do to us. Imagine everyone walking around shar-

ing WOW! What would the world be
like if this were everyone's rule of con-
duct? No person can truly experience
the exhilaration of WOW unless he
translates the Golden Rule into action
and shares WOW with others.

There are limitless ways to share WOW. There are
limitless ways to help others recognize and utilize
their potential. Whenever you help others feel good
about themselves and positive about their future, you
are sharing WOW. Whenever you help someone
realize his true abilities rather than his imagined in-
abilities, you are sharing WOW. The spirit of sharing
WOW has no limit.

Another way to share WOW is to acknowledge and
appreciate others for the good they bring to your life.
Begin by simply smiling brightly and saying, *"WOW,
it's good to see you!"* This statement is a powerful gift;
it inspires the recipient.

I saw a bumper sticker that said, *"If only I was who
my dog thinks I am."* Dogs have no problem saying,
"WOW, it's good to see you!" Why should you?

WOW is a highly contagious emotion. The more WOW you give, the more WOW you'll have to give. Start right now to share what you are learning about the remarkable nature of being human. This attitude has WOW written all over it.

The law of Multiple Returns

The Law of Multiple Returns states that what you put out in the world comes back multiplied. If you plant an apple seed, it becomes an apple tree bearing hundreds of apples. When you plant WOW in the world, you not only share your enthusiasm, you also put yourself in a position to receive generously from others. Furthermore, there is always an internal return, which makes you a stronger person.

When you plant WOW in the world, you not only share your enthusiasm, you also put yourself in a position to receive the generosity of others.

True guidance comes to those who follow the universal laws of nature. Will you be one of them? I give you full credit for being intelligent, but I do want to bring to your attention that the Law of Multiple Returns functions reciprocally. Therefore, you cannot afford to share with others what you do not want to experience yourself. Do not be led astray by any inclination to share NO and WOE.

Teacher: *Look for ways to share WOW.*

Student: *I'm not sure I have any WOW to share.*

Teacher: *Stop doubting and begin sharing; you will find that you have more WOW than you imagine.*

WOW is like a treasure, half hidden in everyone's field of consciousness. Perhaps you go through your day without noticing it, but it's never totally out of your sight. Everyone catches the occasional glimpse of WOW. When you share it, it becomes glaringly obvious to you.

When we catch folks doing things wrong and say, "NO," we become a harming force in the world. This energy attracts NO's into our lives. This is the spirit of anger and fear.

When we catch folks doing things right and say, "WOW," we are a healing force. This energy attracts WOW's. When benevolent with WOW, we experience compassion for the confusion that others are experiencing. This is the essence of brotherly love.

> **Student:** *What would the world be like if everyone made it a habit to catch others doing things right, and say, "WOW"?*
>
> **Teacher:** *We'd all experience a deep sense of richness in human kindness by seeing the beauty in each other.*

On occasion, I find that my wife believes in me more than I believe in myself. The WOW she shares with me becomes contagious, and soon I believe in myself, anew. I experience this when writing and feeling stuck.

I believe there is a violation of rights in any educational system where the children spend the better part of their youth being exposed to NO more than to the power of WOW. Children's talents and potential are realized or unrealized by their right use or their ignorance of the power of WOW. I believe WOW should be shared in every classroom with every student.

The attitude of WOW is not subtle. It's an indescribable source of light energy that moves mountains. It's a powerful means of persuasion. It brightens everyone's life. Who would deny an enthusiastic experience of de-emphasizing NO and emphasizing YES when setting a lofty goal? A conscious act of goodness is one in which there is no regret.

Student: *What if I don't share WOW?*

Teacher: *When you share WOW outwardly, you flourish inwardly, which is the key to flourishing outwardly. When you don't share wow you don't flourish.*

It's possible

Something extraordinary exists in you.

Never forget this.

Your extraordinary essence wants to express –
don't interfere.

When your woeful attitude plummets to zero,
you become your own hero.

When WOW soars, your hidden talents roar.

*When your woeful attitude
plummets to zero, you become
your own hero.*

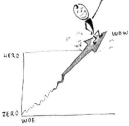

Make your dreams the blueprints for your future by
imbuing them with WOW.

It's possible.

Flares

I will end this chapter with some useful flares that I shoot in the air to help me remember my powerful nature. The flares illuminate the truth, which reminds me of my unlimited possibilities.

I saw a movie where campers were being harassed by howling wolves. One camper shot a flare into the air, and the wolves fled. Here are useful flares that I use to expose NO when it begins howling.

* * *

FLARE #1:

 I can unlearn what I've mistakenly learned.

Just pondering this wisdom gives me a feeling of WOW. With my attitude elevated, I can clearly see that when I set out to **unlearn a teaching of NO**, the attitude of WOE lets go.

* * *

FLARE #2:

NO impairs my view of what's right for me.

Simply accepting this fact gives me a feeling of WOW. Moreover, with an uplifting attitude of WOW, I naturally know what's right – feeling capable of achieving my dreams. When I let this feeling of rightness settle in, it illuminates the lies of NO … and WOE lets go.

FLARE #3:

Don't wait for time to heal my feeling of discouragement – it cannot and will not.

The feeling of discouragement has no power except the power I grant it. When I stop granting it power, I immediately experience WOW. The lingering feeling of discouragement fades … as WOE lets go. It's easy to disobey the urge to hesitate, when WOE lets go.

When I was gullible, I cooperated with NO. These flares help me extricate myself from the senseless drama that NO's impose. Living a life of drama is just wrong. When you feel the wrongness, fire off a flare.

Create your own flares. Allow the flares to illuminate a truth that helps you make right corrections. It would do you good to leaf back through this chapter when creating your own flares. I find that I never get a full understanding of what I've read on the first pass through. Commit to becoming thoroughly acquainted with the power of WOW. Ask, *"What does this have to do with me?"* You will find there is much to learn between the lines.

You now know the power of WOW. It's essential to set yourself free so you may design your earthly destiny as you want it to be. You are finally ready to look directly at the one final thing that stops you from moving mountains in your life ….. the *Counterfeit Self.*

SIX

The Counterfeit Self

The imposter

If it were easy to grasp the concept of an imposter taking over your life, I would not have written the first half of this book to prepare you for this. I would have simply spoken about the *Counterfeit Self* in a simple sentence, as I did earlier, and left it at that.

This imposter, to whom I refer as the *Counterfeit Self*, does not want you looking directly at him; he does not want to be exposed to the light of truth. Like a vampire, he shuns the light

because he doesn't want you to see the horrible truth about him, which is that he is flawed in many ways.

The *Counterfeit Self* convinces you that he is the genuine part of you. He knows you intimately so he is well equipped to deceive you. Millions of human beings act from this false version of themselves while believing they are acting from their authentic nature.

On the façade of the temple of Delphi, in Greece, is written the dictum: "Know Thyself." Well, it seems there are *two selves* to know. One is the original you, with its incredible potential, and the other is the imposter – the *Counterfeit Self*. You created this false version of you during childhood moments of fear and pain. This self is a holographic image of the collection of wrong opinions that you hold as true about you. It's not real, but it feels damn real!

There are two selves to know.

The *Counterfeit Self* lives as an out-picturing of one's internal self-image. This self-image is projected outwardly by the mind. This image is comprised of a collection of wrong thoughts, and when it projects outward, it vandalizes one's life by making wrong choices of action.

It's as if you said, after hearing several thousand NO's: *"I'm going to become a physical expression of the flawed image I hold of myself. I am going to do this by inventing a false version of myself and carrying it with me throughout my life. And I'm going to let it dictate my behavior. I will convince myself, and the world, that it is the real me, even though it is an illusion. Let's get on with the show!"*

The *Counterfeit Self* is the self that represents you when you are feeling insecure and inadequate. On the other hand, there is an incredible power that comes to you when you come to know the *Authentic Self.*

> **Teacher:** *Once the* Counterfeit Self *gets a foothold in your mind and in your life, it does its best to keep you from getting even a glimpse of the* Authentic Self.
>
> **Student:** *How does it do this?*
>
> **Teacher:** *By insisting that it is the authentic you.*

This imposter, passing itself off as you, does you great injustice and causes you to suffer great harm. I've come to know the *Counterfeit Self* so well that when it comes to visit, I say, *"Hello. I know not what kind of harm you've come to do, but I shall have no part of it."*

Its essence

The *Counterfeit Self* gets its power from the conditioned mind. It feeds on thought patterns of NO that support feelings of insecurity and deficiency. Its essence is the belief in insufficiency. By the time we reach young adulthood, the *Counterfeit Self* has had nearly as many birthdays as we've had. As you become aware of its existence, you will recognize the chaos it has wrought in your life.

Only when you succeed at being your *Authentic Self*, can you truly succeed at being happy. Only when you succeed at expressing your original nature, do you really succeed in any domain of your life, be it in business, relationship matters, spiritual matters, you name it. Every great leader must succeed at being authentic first. Real success requires authenticity.

> *Only when you succeed at being your Authentic Self, can you truly succeed at being happy.*

Being authentic and living your own life requires that you know your own mind and follow your own direction. The *Authentic Self* has you feeling confident and sufficient to take command. It's your job to discard the *self* that wastes your time by interfering with your efforts to improve yourself.

You always know which *self* is demonstrating through your personality. One laments WOE and the other exalts WOW. NO and WOE are the *Counterfeit Self's* two favorite expressions. YES and WOW are the *Authentic Self's* favorites.

Two levels

You've read this far in the book, and so I'm confident that you are prepared to look directly at the lower level *self* that you've created. Perhaps you felt like you had little to do with it coming into this world; however, now you know that you had a lot to do with its creation and you have everything to do with how much longer it will possess you. Will you accept this as true?

 To succeed at being authentic, you must be willing to climb to higher levels of living. Your original nature loves climbing upward toward a richer sense of unity and harmony with everything that is evolving in the universe. Are you willing to accept this about you?

You are made to ascend above the flight/fight world of the animal kingdom. When you set the achievement bar higher, you open a small portal in your mind that lets in psychological sunshine. In the light of this sunshine, you can see that you are much stronger than life's struggles. You begin an incredible journey when you know that you're here to experience your personal power.

I believe there are two levels of mental vibration in your mind. Each level offers you a different experience of the world. When being authentic, you access the higher level of mental vibration and elevate your consciousness above the fight/flight reactions found in the animal kingdom.

The *Counterfeit Self* is a low-level thinker – it thrives on lower level vibrations of the mind where NO and WOE exist. That's why it plays it safe and never tries anything new. It avoids being rebuffed or criticized at any cost. It gets its thrills by hanging with cawing crows. It believes it's stupid to be curious and ambitious. Crippling worry runs rampant through its belief system.

Let's take a moment and float back to the past to learn more about the origin of the *Counterfeit Self*.

A quick look back

Do you remember those childhood days when you felt passionate about life, when you ran through the kitchen, squealing with delight? Then someone bigger said, *"NO! Stop that!"* What did you do? You did what every child does; you stopped rejoicing in your curious and ambitious nature. Do you remember what happened next? You experienced an uneasy feeling about yourself for the first time.

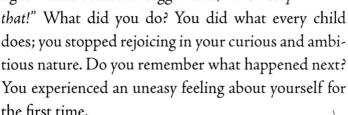

You dismissed the first few NO's, but they persisted, and you became self-conscious. You began feeling uneasy about yourself. You began feeling flawed after hearing so many NO's. What did you do? You began manifesting your inner thoughts of imperfection outwardly; you invented a false version of yourself. This invented *self* is a much-diminished version of your true nature, but you didn't recognize this. Many adults still don't.

It's not over yet. What happened when you began attending school? You met a large gathering of children, just like you, and you felt the urge to sing and dance with them, as did they with you. However, quickly you were taught to curb your enthusiasm, sit still, be quiet and pay attention to the teacher (a person with authority who was loaded with NO's).

You now became even more self-conscious. You began suppressing your playful curiosity to get the teacher's approval. It wasn't long after that, that you totally forgot your authentic nature. You assumed an invented identity and believed that this was all there was to you.

While living as this diminished version of you, it's easy to become self-conscious and embarrassed when trying something new. You pay a hefty price when you begin feeling self-conscious; your potential remains unrealized, and your talents remain hidden, which further validates your false feelings of inadequacy.

Self-consciousness is the ultimate contrivance that the *Counterfeit Self* uses to dominate you. Imagine if you could recall that tragic moment when you first lost sight of the *Authentic Self*, the first time you felt nervously self-conscious; I think you'd sigh and say, "What a mistake!"

Every child suspects that things aren't as they are supposed to be when he first feels ill at ease and self-conscious. However, facing the onslaught of repeated NO's, he assumes, eventually, that this feeling is valid. Take a moment and reflect on how much this errone-ous assumption has cost you.

It's a matter of Cause and Effect

Understanding the makeup of a child's personality is simple; it's a matter of cause and effect. NO's cause the child to feel unsure about himself, and WOE's cause him to feel insecure in the world. And now his personality reflects it.

Take a moment, breathe deeply, and grasp the significance of what you are learning about this kind of human lunacy. We allow a weak, insecure version of ourselves to overwhelm our strong, resourceful nature by nervously anticipating howling NO's, and becoming self-conscious.

Now hear the good news. You have the ability to correct whatever prevents you from having a clear view of the real you. You are endowed with the prerogative to be the cause of the effects you experience in life.

Now that you know that you've been living with not one, but two of you (a healthy and natural *self* and an unhealthy and unnatural *self*) … and now that you know that, when the unhealthy *self* takes control, your attitude slides from WOW to WOE … and now that you know that you are the cause of the effects you experience in life – what will you do about it?

Be patient; opportunities for self rescue are available. Perhaps a tiger can't change its stripes, but you can change the quali- ties of personality that support the false  version of you. You can exercise your privilege of choice. There is no rigid rule that says you must live with this assumed identity.

Nothing is more exhilarating than rediscovering the *Authentic Self*. Nothing is more invigorating than un- covering your remarkable qualities. Your firm decision to do so will reflect in your demean- or, in the way you speak, and in the renewed sparkle in your eyes.

The self to which the ancient Greek aphorism, *Know Thyself*, is referring, is the *Authentic Self*. This self is at- tuned to powers beyond the reach of the *Counterfeit Self*. You are here to use these powers, not neglect them.

It is time to say No to the *self* that feeds on WOE, the *self* that demands your complete attention by de- manding that you put it first in your life, the self that has claimed title to your life. It's time for you to re- claim title to your life; it's time to put the *Counterfeit Self* out of your life.

When your life is lived by a *self* who has a narrow and discouraged view of life, you are doomed to living a narrow and discouraged life. When your life is lived by a *self* who is enthralled with life's marvelous opportunities, you enjoy living a life of marvelous opportunities. Clear seeing is very freeing.

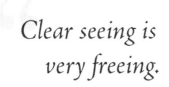

Clear seeing is very freeing.

It's called by many names

The identity thief that corrupts your life is called by many names: the invented self ... the pretender ... the fraudulent self ... the artificial self ... the other self ... the programmed self ... the conditioned self ... the mechanical self ... the false self ... the cheap imitation ... and of course, my personal favorite – the *Counterfeit Self.*

This identity thief has duped you into believing that it is you. You have been duped by an identity that began as a mental concept in childhood moments of hearing NO. Just hearing the above names helps you understand what it really is – an imposter that has stolen your life. One powerful insight is all it takes to motivate a person to make necessary corrections.

> *The Counterfeit Self is an imposter that has stolen your life.*

To submit to the will of the false *self* is to become the slave of a false identity. But simply discovering facts about this *self*, facts of which you were previously unaware, can be incredibly emancipating. By becoming aware of all that's wrong with the *Counterfeit Self*, you have the power of real intelligence; you can invite what's right into your life. Inviting what's right is self-liberating.

Unique perfection or self-corruption

When you look at a newborn baby or a blossoming flower, what do you see? Do you recognize the unique perfection? When you look in the mirror, what do you see? Do you recognize your unique perfection? When you cannot see your own unique perfection, you're participating in the act of self-corruption — the *Counterfeit Self*'s favorite pastime.

Student: *What is the remedy for self-corruption?*

Teacher: *It is the recognition of one's unique perfection.*

When you realize that the *Counterfeit Self* is nothing more than a thought-generated entity, a monster that you created from erroneous self-opinions that you accepted as true while listening to NO, then liberty for the *Authentic Self* becomes your strongest passion and recognizing your unique perfection becomes your greatest value. Wow, that's a mouthful. Read it again, slowly.

If you didn't think the *Counterfeit Self* into existence, it wouldn't be part of you. Moreover, without your cooperation, the *Counterfeit Self* cannot endure. "The fault … lies not in our stars, but in ourselves if we are underlings." -William Shakespeare. Recognize your unique perfection, and the feeling of being an underling disappears.

It's mental madness to participate in self-corruption, which is what you do when you behave as though this *other self* is real.

Mental madness can only attract badness. To be upset with everything bad that happens to you is to separate yourself from the cause of 'cause and effect'. It's not the badness, it's the mental madness that causes wrong choices. Don't delude yourself!

Whenever you find yourself asking, "What On Earth is causing this badness?" take a moment to reflect on what you have just learned. The *Counterfeit Self* chimes in and offers up a thousand excuses why bad things happen to good people like you. If you take the bait, the trap is sprung, suppressing those talents that are unequivocally yours, talents that would verify your unique perfection.

Your progress is an unfolding, like a rose bud; be patient.

Thought-voices

The mind not only remembers past NO's, it also absorbs the disheartening tone of voice that spoke the NO. This tone becomes a thought-voice that is stored in your memory. The *Counterfeit Self* seizes every opportunity to call forth thought-voices that summon unhappy memories. Unfortunately, these voices sound painfully real.

Whenever you consider something fresh and new and a disheartening thought-voice laughs at you, that's the *Counterfeit Self* in action - right there! Until you learn to think at a level higher than memory, these voices will weaken your resolve to try anything new.

The *Counterfeit Self* relies on disheartening thought-voices to control you. Can you see where disheartening thought-voices have dragged you down to lower plateaus of living? Being conscious of this is pure gold.

Becoming conscious
of disheartening
thought-voices
is pure gold.

There are ways to turn down the volume on a disheartening thought-voice, but one thing you do not want to do is resent them. Resentment is a weak quality of character; the *Counterfeit Self* feeds on it. Resentment raises the volume of the voices, which gives you a clenched jaw and a headache. Instead, drop the resentment. Now the mind quiets, and your attitude shifts, and now you can think beyond what the thought-voices suggest.

A great way to drop resentment is to convert the resentment energy into curiosity – a desire to learn more about the nature of these disheartening thought-voices. They are an essential part of unhappy memories. If you've gotten this far in the book, then you have a dozen ways to deal with unhappy memories.

> **Student:** *What's one way that I can deal with my resentment toward disheartening thought-voices?*
>
> **Teacher:** *These voices are trying to haunt you with unhappy memories of past failures, so ask yourself, "Do I believe in ghosts?"*

Any question that helps you break a negative tendency, like resentment, is a healthy question. It doesn't even have to make a lot of sense. Here's another method I use to remain alert to disheartening voices that take over my inward self-talk. I call it the talk-radio method.

Talk-radio method

I consider my inner self-talk as if it were my own personal talk-radio show. I turn on the show when I awaken in the morning and I listen to it until I fall asleep at night. I consider myself the producer of my talk-radio show. This metaphor helps me monitor my inward self-talk.

 Simply noticing the constant chatter helps me understand how popular this talk-radio show is with me. I notice that when I'm mentally lazy, the *Counterfeit Self* becomes the host of my talk-radio show, and it interviews its favorite guests. The guests are the authoritative voices of people from my past that said, "NO!"

One of the *Counterfeit Self's* guests makes me feel guilty, while another makes me feel helpless, and still another makes me feel unworthy, and yet another makes me anxious. As producer of my talk-radio show, my goal is to ban disheartening voices from the air.

 When the *Counterfeit Self* is hosting, it broadcasts nothing but false information about me. If the show were aired publicly, I could sue for defamation of

character. Of course, I'm aware that I'm the one that hands the microphone over to the *Counterfeit Self* and its invited guests. If I really want to unplug the microphone, I need only change the inner conversations that I have with myself.

Another problem occurs when I allow the *Counterfeit Self* to host my talk-radio show; it increases its sphere of influence to include the control of my mental movie theater. It plays only the movies that it enjoys, which are all the reruns of past failures that support its demoralizing diatribes.

Looking at the *Counterfeit Self* and its band of un-merry thought-voices this way, helps me realize how reckless I've been with my inward self-talk. It also helps me to understand how the *Counterfeit Self* will resort to any method it can to stop me from climbing to higher plateaus of living.

It's harmful to deceive myself into thinking that I can both listen to negative self-talk and live a happy, successful life. When I catch myself listening to discouraging inner voices, I say, *"Do I really want to listen to this? It's time to reclaim control of my talk-radio show."*

This puts a smile on my face and creates the space for me to take my self-talk in a new direction.

Do you like this talk-radio show method of silencing the *Counterfeit Self* when it takes over your inward self-talk? Then use it. Use whatever works. Awareness is potential power; but when you act on what you have learned, you wield the actual power.

I also use parables to help deepen my understanding of the *Counterfeit Self*, so I can rid myself of it.

Orphaned eagle parable

Life lessons are often easier to accept when we hear them without self-reference. Of course, the next step is to ask, *"What does this have to do with me?"* Here is a parable that has helped me view my own two *selves.*

 A farmer found an orphaned eagle in a field and placed him in the chicken coop. The young eagle began identifying with the chickens and started imitating their ways. The eagle assumed an identity based on a mistaken mind-concept; it was contrary to his instincts, but he choose to believe it over his inner urge to soar high in the sky.

Consequently, the eagle turned this mistaken concept into reality. He began pecking at the ground for scraps and clucking like a nervous chicken.

One day an older eagle flew over and witnessed this peculiar sight. It swooped down and cornered the young eagle. The older eagle spoke of the young eagle's authentic nature and completed the conversation with this: "There are no limitations placed on your life as an eagle, except those intimidations you've imposed upon yourself."

> *There are no limitations placed on your life except those intimidations you've imposed upon yourself.*

The young eagle immediately stopped clucking like a nervous chicken and reacted rightly to this rescuing message. It took but a moment before it rejected its false identity and soared high into the open sky.

How has your assumed identity stopped you from soaring? How has it left you pecking for scraps? With what mistaken mental concepts do you intimidate yourself? What limitations have you placed on yourself?

 It's time to react rightly to the rescuing truth. It's time to return to the open sky. I have a photo of an eagle in my office to remind me of this.

How will you use this parable to better your life? There is a part of you that is perfectly capable of soaring. Listen to that part of you.

> **Student:** *Why does the* Counterfeit Self *try to stop me from soaring to higher plateaus of living?*
>
> **Teacher:** *Because higher soaring gives you right sight, and the first thing you see is that you've victimized yourself by assuming a false identity.*

There are many ways to remind yourself that you are more than the limitations you've imposed on yourself. Finding the appropriate reminder is an individual matter, and now I offer you my *plastic pear* reminder. Perhaps it will help you find a reminder that will work for you.

Plastic pear reminder

I have a plastic pear on my desk in my study. This piece of artificial fruit looks amazingly real, but the difference between biting into this dry imitation and biting into a ripe, juicy pear is extraordinary.

This plastic pear reminds me that the *Counterfeit Self* is no more authentic than plastic fruit. It reminds me of the extraordinary difference between the artificial version of me and my authentic nature.

The plastic pear puts up a fabulous false front. The *Counterfeit Self* puts up a fabulous false front. The plastic pear has no real value. The *Counterfeit Self* has no real value. The plastic pear is a cheap imitation. The *Counterfeit Self* is a cheap imitation. The plastic pear reminds me that I have temporarily misplaced my sanity when I give any credence to the *Counterfeit Self*'s suggestions.

Is there a piece of plastic fruit in your house somewhere? It is ready to help you whenever you're ready.

To whom will you listen?

E.E. Cummings said, "To be nobody but yourself in a world that's doing its best to make you somebody else is to fight the hardest battle you are ever going to fight. Never stop fighting." Might I add that the fight to be nobody but yourself is made more difficult when you listen to the confusing and demoralizing advice of the *Counterfeit Self*. Never underestimate your ability to win the battle, no matter how difficult it may seem.

Popeye the Sailor Man would gulp a can of spinach and say, "I yam what I yam and that's all what I yam." Popeye's resolute acceptance of this fact enabled him to live consciously from his values rather than mechanically from a false version of himself.

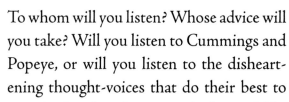 To whom will you listen? Whose advice will you take? Will you listen to Cummings and Popeye, or will you listen to the disheartening thought-voices that do their best to make you somebody other than your *Authentic Self?*

It's because of disheartening thought-voices, that you built this robotic being, the *Counterfeit Self*, and programmed it to react mechanically to NO. It's time to be nobody but yourself. It's time to dismantle the robot. You will win the battle. Great achievers are those who see the value of being an original rather than a mechanical imitation.

A noble act

The *Counterfeit Self* is a complex force of energy that is cruel to you. It's a noble act to take inventory of the many ways the *Counterfeit Self* attacks, and then move to remove this force from its position of prominence in your life.

How's your immune system – do you get colds easily?

How's your temperament – are you moody?

How are you sleeping – are you restless at night?

How are your relationships – are they filled with melodrama?

How are your finances – do you struggle with money?

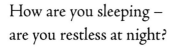

The above are but a few of the ways that the *Counterfeit Self* tyrannizes you. You can learn from what is true, or you can let your false identity burn you.

> *You can learn from what is true, or you can let your false identity burn you.*

The *Counterfeit Self* is like an onion with layers and layers of NO and WOE. The layers cause nightmares. When you peel away the layers, you come to the core, and, like an onion, there's nothing there. See this as a way to understand that the *Counterfeit Self* is a giant hoax.

The false version of you is dull and wearisome; it engraves itself on your face and on the way you carry yourself. This false version of you is over-reactive, is rigid and insecure, is physically exhausting, and is based on lies. It encourages minimal living because its essence is fear. What could be a nobler act than to rid yourself of this fabrication that poses as real?

Now let's look at the *Authentic Self.* You are radiant and cheerful, infinitely unique and superlatively creative and incredibly resourceful. Your potential is unlimited, and your spirit is rejuvenating. This *self* encourages optimal living because its essence is peaceful and loving, ambitious and curious. What could be a nobler act than to open your arms to what is true?

Those who do not observe the movements of the *Counterfeit Self* must of necessity be disappointed with their lives. The moment you *"Know Thyself"* (thy real self), a deep peaceful silence comes over you. Let what's real about you shake you loose from your false identity.

Startling revelation

It's a startling revelation to see the *Counterfeit Self* as a useless invention that confines you to a dull, boring world. There is absolutely nothing about this *self* that is satisfying, other than the comfort that comes with familiarity. It's time, say, "Sayonara." Be daring, unplug the robot, step into the unfamiliar, let your spirit soar.

There is absolutely nothing about the Counterfeit Self *that is satisfying, other than the comfort that comes with familiarity.*

Chapter by chapter you've grown more and more familiar with the truth about yourself; it's time to return home to your original nature. It matters not how far you've strayed; delay no longer.

> **Student:** *What can I expect if I return home to my original nature?*
>
> **Teacher:** *It may feel dizzying at first, but soon you will feel fully engaged with life in significant ways because finally you will start living your life and stop living the lies.*

There is a remarkably effective way to start living your life and stop living the lies .... Call an MD!

SEVEN

Marvelous Denials

Ending self delusion

Now that you can see that the *Counterfeit Self* is nothing more than a negative abstraction that you have put into action, you can end its reign over your life. The only way to achieve this is to end the self delusion that comes with listening to old NO's. Use the pain of delusion as a signal for turning to what is true and best for you.

When you can see the Counterfeit Self as nothing more than a negative abstraction that you have put into action, you can end its reign over your life.

 It's during one's vulnerable years that he creates, nurtures, and identifies with the *Counterfeit Self.* You are no longer that vulnerable child. You are aware of the many bad decisions this *other self* has made for you. Are you ready for a change?

Unfortunately, what you identify with, you become. However, there is a way out, a way to *dis-identify* with this crafty culprit. You are about to learn a method to rid yourself of this negative abstraction. You cannot make right decisions that advance your life, until your inner world is a place where the *Counterfeit Self* cannot survive.

Be always the commander in chief, when it comes to your mind, and the *Counterfeit Self* shall harm you no longer.

Student: *What stops me from simply dis-identifying with this false self?*

Teacher: *It's easy to blame the world for your problems, and that's what you do. It takes courage to face the truth by looking inward, and that's what you need to do.*

Inward investigation

The mind is a marvelous tool when used properly. It wreaks havoc with one's life when used improperly. One evening, while sitting in my office and calmly reflecting on how well things were going, I suddenly became overcome with worry about my newest real estate project. I began thinking that I'd taken on more than I could handle, given the slump in the market. In a matter of moments, I was deluged with worry.

Fortunately, there was a corner of my consciousness that was noticing what was happening without getting emotionally involved. It dawned on me that it was time to investigate something I'd been suspecting for years – that I was still holding on to a collection of highly charged opinions about lacking the ability to achieve my highest ambitions.

Everyone has a large collection of opinions stored in the subconscious vault of his mind. Some are obviously apparent and some are invisible. The invisible ones can be treacherous because they affect our attitude and mood without our knowing it.

It occurred to me that my *Counterfeit Self* had snuck down to the studio vault and was playing back an old soundtrack from my childhood days when I feared poverty. This soundtrack was being played at a frequency that I could not hear, but clearly it was affecting me adversely. By simply listening carefully, I realized that my doubt was arising from a conversation that my father had with me after losing the little money he'd managed to save. He said, "Bobby, don't take risks with money or you'll lose it."

By making myself conscious of this soundtrack, I understood why I'd slid from an attitude of WOW (thinking well of myself and appreciating my real estate project) to an attitude of WOE (thinking against myself and fearing the loss of money), and it happened in a matter of moments.

On this particular evening I decided to stop playing games with myself. I'd already spent a year investigating my *two selves,* so now it was time to do something with this knowledge. I asked myself, *"Which self is expressing through me right now?"* It was apparent that I was expressing a *'WOE is me'* tendency, which is always a liability. It was also clear that this liability is the consequence of a negative quality possessed by the *Counterfeit Self.*

The way to making right changes always begins with awareness of wrongness. Without awareness, it's impossible to make corrections. I asked myself a healthy question: *"How can I create space for my Authentic Self to express through my personality?"* The answer came quickly. *"I must sensitize my attention to nay-saying thought-voices and negative soundtracks that give life to the Counterfeit Self."* Then I asked, *"And when I catch this happening, what should I do?"* Out of nowhere, I heard myself shout,

"Call an MD!"

Student: *What's an MD?*

Teacher: *It's a Marvelous Denial... deny the lies!*

Awaken to a world of appreciation

There is no better way to awaken to a world of appreciation than to call an **MD** when your lie becomes worrisome.

1. Call an **MD** – to deny the faulty lies of discouraging thought-voices that make you feel inadequate.

2. Call an **MD** – to deny the opinions that come from alarming soundtracks of your past; opinions make you feel insecure.

3. Call an **MD** – to deny the validity of all ideas that make you feel unworthy of experiencing a wonderful life.

4. Call an **MD** – to deny all fictional self-talk that gives strength to NO and WOE.

If you call **MD's** regularly, you make the most **M**arvelous **D**enial of all:

You deny the reality of the *Counterfeit Self.*

Marvelous Denials feel marvelous because they reject the *Counterfeit Self,* they mute its un-merry band of thought voices, and they lock the door to its library of discouraging soundtracks. When you solve these problems, you can solve all of your problems. How marvelous is that?

Make it a habit

You are about to take a sales course. You are going to learn how to engage in the art of persuasion – not to persuade others, but, rather, to persuade your own mind. The intent of an **MD** is to persuade your mind to listen to you, not to the *Counterfeit Self*.

Imagine making a habit of calling an **MD** whenever it's needed. When calling an **MD** is a habit, you can  relax because you've convinced the subconscious level of your mind to automatically reject any opinion that does not benefit you. How do you make calling an **MD** a habit? Here are four easy steps:

1. Create a ritual while calling an **MD**…
    I snap my fingers.

2. Be enthusiastic when calling an **MD**…
    enthusiasm is a quality of energy that
    sells convincingly; it convinces the
    subconscious level of your mind to listen.

3. Call an **MD** with conviction and
persistence. Be patient. The mind
succumbs to repetition.

4. Express gratitude after calling an **MD**…
Say, *"Thank you,"* for the benefits you will
receive for creating this habit pattern.

Your mind belongs exclusively to you. You are its
commander in chief, both at the conscious and subconscious level of thinking. Be fearless when calling an MD and you will be invincible when you get
backlash from the *Counterfeit Self.* The more you take
command, the more persuasive you are when dealing
with the subconscious level of your mind, which is
where habit patterns take root.

You can train your mind to think as you
want it to think. If your mind is going to
be bound by fixed patterns of thought,
then you should decide what they will be.
Remind yourself of this daily. It is invigo-
rating to know this.

The purpose of repeatedly calling an **MD** is to sweep the basement of your mind free of all those NO's. When the basement is swept clean, the mind is free of harmful conditioning, and the *Counterfeit Self* flees. Now the bright truth works its cure on your unhealthy attitude.

Calling an **MD** is a positive act. It's always healthy to challenge harrowing opinions with the intention of dismissing them. Even the most disciplined mind occasionally goes astray, and the best course of action is conscious intervention – call an **MD**. All great achievers call **MD**'s in their unique way.

Abe Lincoln began his political career as an awkward country lawyer. He didn't become one of America's most renowned presidents without intervening when his mind began howling with NO's. He called **MD**'s in his unique way when dealing with bouts of depression throughout his illustrious career. Look at what he accomplished.

There is no better way to a render a defeat temporary than to call an **MD** on the lies that make succeeding seem impossible. Self-reliance begins when you begin denying the lies that dishearten you. With conscious intervention, you find yourself acting rightly toward your defeats, rendering even the most difficult ones temporary.

Never avoid facing those opinions that pull your attitude down into the depths of WOE. Look right at them and deny their validity. Your aim is to end the emotional turmoil they cause. Calling an **MD** is a vital step toward all meaningful success. No one experiences a meaningful triumph on the first try; the secret to success is to call an **MD**, and try again.

An **MD** is an indispensable tool when developing one's mind beyond its mechanically reactive tendency. The first step is to begin to suspect that you may be far more mechanically reactive than you realize. If you feel offended in any way by this statement, know this: Feeling offended is the *Counterfeit Self's* trick to discourage you from suspecting that you're mechanically reactive.

The ultimate lie to deny

Might I repeat again that the *Counterfeit Self* is the ultimate lie to deny. When I committed to denying the validity of this *Self*, I found myself questioning every belief I held about myself. My intention was to make corrections that would separate me from this faker.

I decided that if I'm going to be *self-conscious*, let me be *conscious* of the *self* that is authentically me, not the faker. I could see that I was being gullible whenever I began listening to a thought-voice that would say, *"NO, you're being foolish; stop thinking you can change what is so … and what is so is the flawed self that you are destined to live with."* This voice would rudely demand that I quit this self-improvement endeavor at once, and get on with my life.

I decided that if I'm going to be self-conscious, let me be conscious of the self that is authentically me, not the faker.

I began catching myself listening to discouraging thought-voices, and I knew right then that it was time for me to reprioritize my values. It was time to place self-approval high on my priority list and take self-reproach off the list. One great value breathed into a person's soul can regenerate him.

> *One great value breathed into a person's soul can regenerate him.*

It was easy to ignore taunting thought-voices when I denied the lies they offered and resolved to see myself as a remarkable being with extraordinary qualities. I find that an inspiring attitude always brings out the best in me.

Reminding myself of my remarkableness inspired me to call an **MD** whenever the *Counterfeit Self* took over my talk-radio show. I would say to myself, *"I am fully capable of controlling my car radio, and I am just as capable of controlling my inward self-talk radio show."* It was apparent to me that no one else can call an **MD** for me, nor should you expect anyone to call one for you.

Calling an **MD** sets up a special kind of communication between you and your mind. It not only awakens you to your *Authentic Self*, it enables you to communicate this *self* to your mind.

Controlling your point of concentration

Calling an **MD** is not crying out, beseeching or pleading for help. This is behavior that strengthens the *Counterfeit Self*. The secret to calling an effective **MD** is to control your point of concentration, to bring your mind to focus on one thing and forget everything else.

> **Student:** *What's the one thing I want my mind to concentrate on?*

> **Teacher:** *The truth about your incredible potential as a human being.*

> **Student:** *What's the 'everything else' that I want it to forget?*

> **Teacher:** *The lies that prevent it from focusing on your incredible potential.*

Lack of concentration sabotages your chances of succeeding in life. When you control your point of concentration, you shift your allegiance from WOE to WOW. This is because you begin noticing remarkable things about yourself that become valuable assets to your growth and development.

Take time every morning to vow that you will not act in ways today that please the *Counterfeit Self,* so it is pleased with you. If this *self* is pleased with your action, the odds are your action is inappropriate and harmful to you. Instead, control your point of concentration upon all of the things that the *Counterfeit Self* will insist are not true about you.

If you're going to call an effective **MD**, you've got to get both your head and your heart into it. You are calling an **MD** to interfere with self-talk that offers faulty opinions about you. You are exposing the lies in order to feel the proper self-reverence and self-respect that you deserve.

You are doing this so you can be your own *center of influence* for your own good. You are doing something very important for yourself. You are helping yourself find your own unique qualities that support successful living.

Whenever you deny the lies that you hold about yourself, you call on a healing presence. This presence is the essence of your being; it is your internal healer. This presence is able to heal the deepest psychological wounds.

The illuminating practice of calling an **MD** enables you to distinguish between the source that offers beneficial truth and the source that offers painful deception. It's time to stop making shallow assumptions about yourself. The Bhagavad-Gita says of the person who stops making such shallow assumptions, "He has chosen the highway; he will advance."

If calling an effective **MD** could have been explained in a few pages, I'd not have written an entire book leading up to it.

Choose the highway

When you choose the highway, you see the folly of NO and WOE. Take a moment to acknowledge and appreciate the inner work you're doing right now. You are giving up lies that harm you so you can transmute your dreams into strong convictions that advance you. Keep going!

IT'S TIME FOR A POP QUIZ:

Let's see which self you are being right now.

(**1**) Are you reading this book with an open and receptive mind?

YES _____   NO _____

(**2**) Are you entertaining ideas that your usual nature would reject?

YES _____   NO _____

If the answers to questions 1 & 2 are YES and YES, then the self that is reading is the authentic you; it's the source of your love of growth. If the answers are NO and NO, then it's the *other self* that's reading the book; it's the source of your fear of change.

Choosing the highway elevates your consciousness; it enables you to slip free of confusion and darkness found at lower-level thinking. When you slip free, you see an astonishingly beneficent being – that's you!

FOUR STEPS THAT EMPOWER YOU TO CALL AN MD

It's time for the big event. It's time to learn the steps to take when you catch yourself brooding, feeling discouraged, harshly judging, or emotionally reacting to life. These four steps empower you to successfully call an **MD** and have it be effective.

STEP 1: IMAGINE

Take a moment to turn within. Go into the innermost chamber of your mind where only you can enter. Trust that this chamber exists. It's where you shut out the world.

While in this chamber, imagine a being standing there that is relaxed and easy, and full of vibrant energy. As you approach this being, you realize that it's not a fictional character; it's real; it's really you. Your power to make **M**arvelous **D**enials comes from this vibrant being.

STEP 2:
INTELLIGENT IDENTIFICATION

Now it's time to do the intelligent thing and identify with this being. Refuse to sacrifice your life to old, outdated opinions that stop you from identifying with this being.

You are not on a debating team. Don't argue with yourself to prove you are this essence; simply stretch your mind and open your heart to the truth. Know that you are in the right place and doing the right thing by identifying with this being.

Say to yourself, *"I am this vibrant being, this incredible presence, and it is guiding me to the truth about myself."*

Close your eyes and say this again, *"I am this vibrant being, this incredible presence, and it is guiding me to the truth about myself."* Listen to your words.

STEP 3: MARVELOUSLY DENY

Deny the lie that broke into your mind of its own accord, the thought that had you feeling discouraged, brooding, or acting in a negative fashion.

Don't angrily deny this lie, simply voice your denial in an easy style, with a sincere commitment to understand what is true about you. Deny it with deep conviction.

Speak your denial aloud, so your ears can hear it. *"I deny this negative self-opinion that has broken into my mind. The opinion is a lie, and I grant it no power in my life. Further, I deny the Counterfeit Self power in my life through the act of calling an* **MD** *on this lie."*

Put these words in writing, and take them with you so you don't forget them. If you come up with a statement that works better for you, I encourage you to write it down.

Deny the lie again. *"I deny this negative self-opinion that has broken into my mind. The opinion is a lie, and I grant it no power in my life. Further, I deny the* Counterfeit Self *power in my life through the act of calling an* **MD** *on this lie."* Let the feeling settle in.

STEP 4: FACTS AND ACTS

You have stated the facts in Step 3, and now it's time to act. See yourself taking action that backs up your denial, and act. Don't sit idly waiting for things to happen – make them happen!

Your definite aim with this step is to notice any personality tendency that gives life to the lie you just denied. Now you are doing whatever it takes to curb that tendency from expressing by finding a way to express the opposite behavior.

For example, if you hear yourself saying, *"How stupid of me,"* deny the lie by saying something like this: *"I deny that I'm stupid. This opinion is a lie, and I grant it no power in my life. I am not stupid. I am intelligent. I simply made a mistake and I will use my intelligence to clean up any problem I caused."*

Now prove the above statement to yourself by taking action; make any correction needed to resolve the problem you caused and spend the rest of your day consciously acting in ways that demonstrate your intelligence.

You are acting intelligently for yourself, not for the approval of others. Don't assume that you will always succeed on the first try. Flexibility is one of the qualities of intelligence. The more you practice acting as though you are intelligent, the more you acquaint yourself with your intelligence.

" As the mind is made intelligent, the capacity of the soul for pure enjoyment is proportionately increased." – Lew Wallace

Telling on myself

There was a time when I had a tendency to exaggerate, to add spice to a story so I'd look good. When I realized the damage it did to my relationships, and to my self-esteem, I made it a priority to catch myself exaggerating so I could stop. I'd stop right in the middle of my story, and think to myself, *"I deny the lie that I'm too boring to tell an interesting story. I deny any negative self-opinion that has bolted into my mind and compelled me to exaggerate. The opinion is a lie."*

Saying this to myself took but a second. Then I'd say to the person I was speaking to, *"I'm exaggerating; let me start over."* Wow, admitting this was embarrassing, but I resolved to keep it up until I stopped exaggerating. It worked.

The *Counterfeit Self,* which owned the bad habit of exaggerating, was using the feeling of embarrassment to stop me from correcting myself. When I endured the embarrassment, the *Counterfeit Self* began losing its iron-tight grip on me. I am now able to express myself with the interesting truth less the embellishments. It feels great.

Marvelous Denials offer clarity to your inspiring commitments in life. Every time you call an **MD**, you are better able to clarify the path that you intend your life to take.

You can vanquish the *Counterfeit Self* and its dark ways by calling an **MD** whenever you hear its first faint whispering of NO or WOE, or whenever you find yourself caught up in one of its bad habits. Calling an **MD** clarifies your new position, which is to hold yourself accountable for correcting bad habits that never work in your life.

Beware: NO-Traps

John Steinbeck said, "Man is the only kind of varmint sets his own trap, baits it, then steps in it." The *Counterfeit Self* is the varmint that sets traps, baits them, and then waits for you to step in them. I call them NO-Traps. Beware of NO-Traps whenever you attempt to improve your life.

Your NO-Traps are personal to you and can be found in every domain of life, be it financial, with relationships, or deal-  ing with personal affairs. Whenever you decide to lift your attitude from WOE to WOW, by calling an **MD**, expect a NO-Trap. The purpose of a NO-Trap is to stop you. When a NO-Trap SNAPS, you feel the pain of falling back.

> **Student**: *What's the bait of a NO-Trap?*
>
> **Teacher**: *NO-Traps are falsehoods, cleverly disguising themselves as truths, trying to ensnare you. They are baited with pictures of past failures that reinforce discouraging thought-voices.*

You are working on your own personal *mental management program* right now. Be persistent when call- ing an **MD**; the *Counterfeit Self* doesn't give up eas- ily. You cannot override discouraging thought-voices, and bring your mind to the positive side, until you truly believe that you have the potential to succeed.

When you call an **MD**, you are seeking freedom from emotionalized opinions that ground your ambitious spirit. These emotionalized opinions carry old pictures of past failures as proof of their validity. You must make an unwavering commitment to deny the lies that pictures of past failures and emotionalized opinions offer.

The purpose of your *mental management program* is to convince your mind that there is possibility where it now sees defeat. If this is to be, it is up to thee, and a great way to do this is to call an **MD** whenever doubts creep in to spoil your dreams.

> *If it is to be, it is up to thee.*

Might I tell on myself once again? Here's an example of a NO-Trap that SNAPPED on me when I called an **MD**. Within three days of buying a new car, I was involved in a minor parking lot accident and I was blaming the other driver for not looking while backing up. I caught myself reacting angrily and decided to call an **MD**: *"How absurd of me; I'm getting angry and making a big deal over a minor fender-bender. I deny the lie that feeling bitter and blaming the other driver for the accident is going to solve the problem."*

I barely finished calling the **MD**, when SNAP went a NO-Trap. A past picture of me being passive flashed into my mind. It was an incident that happened a few years  earlier, and because I didn't stand up for myself, I was taken advantage of. Along with this picture came a thought-voice that said, *"Feeling bitter is valid; he wasn't looking where he was going. Do you think you don't have a right to feel resentful and angry?"*

The *Counterfeit Self* was trying to bully me into believing that I was a victim and convince me that reacting angrily was appropriate. Reacting angrily is one of the *Counterfeit Self's* many bad habits.

What had just happened? One small negative incident was enough to bring on a big emotional reaction from the *Counterfeit Self*. When I intervened with an **MD**, I stepped in the NO-Trap, which was set to convince me that things would get worse if I didn't get angry.

When calling an **MD**, the point is to respond from new knowledge, not from old pictures of failure that tumble into one's consciousness. Unfortunately, when we react to one negative opinion, a whole chain of like-kind negative opinions rush forth to reinforce the initial one. These opinions come with more pictures from the past that reinforce the negative point of view. Often, this occurs at the subconscious level, so we're not consciously aware of it. I consider these the traps of which Steinbeck spoke.

Back to my story. I recognized that I'd stepped in a NO-Trap and immediately resolved to solve the matter within myself. I asked the other driver if I might take a moment to calm myself and walk around to the other side of the car. He amiably agreed, and I did just that.

I then called another **MD**. This time I purposely made it electrifying by creating a mental picture of me calmly exchanging papers with the other driver and shaking hands as we parted. With this picture in my mind I said to myself, *"How absurd of me. I'm lying to myself by feeling bitter and thinking that is the best way to solve things. This opinion is a lie, and I grant it no power in my life. Further, I deny the* Counterfeit Self *power in my life through the act of calling an* **MD** *on this lie.*

I was taking a moment to hold myself accountable for resolving my bitter feelings and taking care of this matter in a civil fashion. Consequently, I turned this event into a learning moment, and the matter was handled quickly. We exchanged papers, shook hands and parted.

Positive opinions, like negative opinions, also link together. If you persist in denying the lie with an attitude of WOW, it won't be long before other like-kind positive memories come spilling out to rescue you. Now it's easier to handle matters with dignity and grace, two qualities that are absent in the *Counterfeit Self* and always present in the *Authentic Self*.

Might I offer one more example of a NO-Trap that SNAPPED on me when I called an **MD**? I was thinking about writing my first book but I was also questioning whether I was capable of writing effectively. Did I have the talent? I immediately called an **MD**: *"What kind of nonsense is this? I am shocked at the foolish suggestion that I don't have the talent to write a book."*

I barely called the above **MD**, when SNAP went a NO-Trap. The *Counterfeit Self* interrupted with a discouraging thought-voice, *"Hold on now, look at the absurdity*

of this aspiration. *You would have to learn to write, go to writer's workshops, and take classes before you could write a book that isn't just gobbledygook.*" And there I was, staring at a past picture of me, feeling resigned and upset after getting a poor grade in a creative writing course I'd taken in college.

This discouraging picture was accompanied by a choir of discouraging voices that chimed in with false evidence to prove the insanity of this book-writing aspiration: "*I'm too busy. I'm too old. I'm just not that talented when it comes to writing.*" I knew by now that I had to take the time to think for myself and act from new knowledge, not from an old picture of what happened decades ago. Perhaps the NO-Trap snapped, but I knew how to set myself free.

 I called another **MD** in a way that inspired me, "*It's too late? WOW, someone should have told Grandma Moses that when she took up painting. How ridiculous! Enough of this sad sack act! I see how the* Counterfeit Self *is trying to lure me into an emotional tornado with that old picture of me failing at writing. The opinion that I'm not talented at writing is a lie, and I grant it no power in my*

life. Further, I deny the Counterfeit Self *power in my life through the act of calling an* **MD** *on this lie."*

I then took the time to create a mental picture of me at a book-signing event at a local bookstore. I put a big bright smile on my face in the picture and added bright vibrant colors to the scene. Just doing this replenished my enthusiasm. We always feel better when we discover deceptive opinions and deny their validity. That scene of me holding a book at a signing event came true; it was a whopping success.

One of the healthiest things you can do is to stop NO-Traps from ensnaring you. Remember what the teacher said: NO-Traps are falsehoods, cleverly disguising themselves as truths, to ensnare you. NO-Traps cannot ensnare you, unless you allow them to, and that's what you do when you wail out, "Poor me!"

It is remarkably useful to endure any uncomfortable feeling that comes with hearing the SNAP of a NO-Trap. Let the uncomfortable feeling remind you that old pictures of past failures and discouraging thought-voices are in violation of natural law, and that's why they feel uncomfortable.

Student: *What's life like when the SNAP of a NO-Trap no longer ensnares you?*

Teacher: *You find yourself exercising good judgment more and more frequently.*

Speak up for yourself

If you are to improve your life, you must be willing to speak up for yourself. Stop pledging your allegiance to illogical opinions that have no basis in reality. It's as easy to believe in super self-sufficiency as it is to believe in self-deficiency. Believing in super self-sufficiency gives you refreshing shivers of enthusiasm. Can you feel the rightness of this?

> *It's as easy to believe in super self-sufficiency as it is to believe in self-deficiency.*

I urge you to come up with your own unique way of calling an **MD**; come up with your own style of dealing with NO-Traps. Tailor your *mental management program* so it works for you. Become quiet about ev-

erything else. Concentrate your attention.
Calling an **MD** is a heroic act.

Be discerning – use intelligent self-talk.

Be innovative – there are thousands
of ways to persuade your mind
that your potential is unlimited.

Be authoritative – mean it.

Be electrifying – speak your **Marvelous
Denials** with enthusiasm.

Be natural – say what comes spontaneously;
put no extraneous effort into it.

Be persistent – don't stop denying the lies
until you feel satisfied that you've reached
the subconscious level of your mind.

Be fearless – it's your birthright to
be yourself.

Be rigorous, while being kind to yourself –
let the SNAP of a NO-Trap remind you of
how foolishly lax you've been.

You feel it when you call the rescuing truth to save
you from old NO's. You experience a superior state of

mind. The qualities of curiosity and ambition come rushing back to you.

There's a big difference

There is a big difference between a **Marvelous Denial** and an unhealthy denial. We usually think of denial as part of the human defense mechanism where we insist a fact is a lie. We do this because the *Counterfeit Self* makes it painful to accept the fact, even if it could help us to grow. This is an unhealthy denial. It causes suffering and misery.

Marvelous Denials are healthy because you are denying the validity of unhealthy opinions that stop you from experiencing WOW. A successful **MD** offers a marvelous feeling. The moment the orphaned eagle **Marvelously Denied** the lie that said he was a chicken, his attitude soared. He then spread his wings and flew high into the open sky.

In the play, *Richard II*, William Shakespeare has a gardener say, "We lop away that bearing boughs may live." When **Marvelously Denying** a lie that has you feeling fragile and helpless, you lop away discouraging thoughts of WOE that productive fruit-bearing boughs of WOW may live in your garden of thoughts. When lopping away discouraging thoughts, you truly do something wise. Take five minutes to reflect on this.

Misleading opinions have been heaped upon you since childhood. You've now had a clinical look at your inventory of opinions. Simply doing this helps you feel the rightness of ridding your belief system of wrong opinions, doesn't it.

You've learned not to harshly judge yourself for what you found. You've learned that if you're going to be judgmental, judge in your own favor by denying the lies that have you harshly judging yourself.

If you're going to be judgmental, judge in your own favor by denying the lies that have you harshly judging yourself.

Here are examples of folks who denied lies that impaired their progress, thereby reaching their incredible potential.

Tom Dempsey denied the lie that insisted he could not be a field goal kicker because he had no toes on his right foot. He gave this lie no credibility and went on to kick the longest field goal in NFL history. If he'd accepted the lie as true, he would have made his handicap a hindrance. Would he have ever made football history?

James Earl Jones denied the lie that insisted his stuttering would stop him from acting. He overcame this speech condition and is now a famous actor of theater and film, best known for his distinctive voice. If he'd accepted the lie as true, would he ever have received an Honorary Academy Award?

Ludwig van Beethoven denied the lie that insisted deafness would end his incredible music-composition

career. If he'd accepted the lie as true, would he have composed his ninth and final symphony in 1824 when he was completely deaf?

Helen Keller contracted an illness that left her deaf and blind at age two. With Annie Sullivan's help, she denied the lie that said she was severely limited. If she accepted the lie, would she have been the first deaf/ blind person to get a Bachelors of Arts degree? Would she have been a world famous author and lecturer?

How's that for making healthy denials?

FOR-GIVE

There is an introspective endeavor that comes with calling an **MD**; it is an act of FOR-GIVE-ing ... you GIVE up an unhealthy opinion FOR the healthy truth. It's a cleansing ritual; you're cleansing your attitude of unhealthy WOES by reclaiming respect for yourself.

If you're to give up your unhealthy opinions, you must question your feelings of insufficiency at every opportunity. Do it with unwavering persistence. This enables you to see clearly that you have great merit, which brings out the best in you. What a great gift you give yourself.

Remember, it's never too late to start living an enriching life. You naturally appreciate the unfolding of a flower; it's time to appreciate your own incredible unfolding. Let this idea make you new!

When I first came up with the idea of calling an **MD**, I came up with the following ways that it could help me:

1. **MD's** teach my mind to GIVE up serving the *Counterfeit Self* FOR serving the authentic me.

2. **MD's** help me GIVE up hurried reactions FOR calm decisions.

3. **MD's** help me GIVE up feeling awkward FOR being poised.

4. **MD's** help me GIVE up compulsive habits FOR organized plans of action.

5. **MD's** help me GIVE up closed-mindedness FOR open-mindedness.

6. MD's help me GIVE up nervousness FOR peacefulness.

7. MD's help me GIVE up believing that failure is a sign of inadequacy FOR flexibility (which includes understanding that failing one's way to success is part of the growing process).

We're back to 'Know Thyself'

You possess many hidden talents. Only when you know thyself can you learn of these talents. Your mind possesses incredible powers. Only when you know thyself can you access these powers.

Socrates' entire philosophy was based on the guiding principle, written on the temple of Delphi. You are training your mind to unlearn the nonsense that stops you from believing what Socrates believed: "Let him that would move the world first move himself."

Thomas Paine said, "Every person of learning is finally his own teacher." You are now ready to be your own teacher. Teach yourself to be yourself; anything less and you stifle yourself, no one else can do this for you.

Value your personal integrity above all else. When you compromise self-integrity, you weaken your resolve to know thyself. This has painful consequences — you've felt them.

Yearn to know the truth about yourself and be willing to do whatever it takes to self-investigate. This book offers momentous truths that can help you to be free to live your life as you want it to be. Begin thinking this way right now. Can you do this? You bet you can!

Your mind is prepared; you are now ready for the *Ultimate Understanding* .....

EIGHT

The Ultimate Understanding

I AM A RICH AND MAJESTIC CHILD
OF INFINITE INTELLIGENCE.

I AM MARVELOUSLY MADE, AND DESTINED
TO WIN AT WHATEVER I SET MY MIND TO,
AND I AM WORTHY OF ALL THAT IS
GOOD AND BEAUTIFUL.

I believe the above revelation is a culmination of man's endless search for something beyond himself. The search is over. The something that we are searching for is an understanding of this incredible truth about ourselves. This is the Ultimate Understanding. It leads us to the *Authentic Self* that lies beyond the *Counterfeit Self*.

If I'd presented you with this statement at the beginning of the book, you would never have understood it as it's meant to be understood. When you come to understand this understanding, it's akin to coming home to yourself; you place yourself on a high level of consciousness that attunes you to many more inspiring truths about your original nature.

You need not understand everything there is to understand about yourself in order to live the glorious life you yearn to experience, but it is important to understand that you are *a rich and majestic child, you are marvelously made, you are destined to win if you set your mind to it, and you are worthy of all that is good and beautiful.*

Truly understanding this revelation gives you the intensifying quality you need to make it part of your deep, subconscious belief system. Now, the rest gets easy; there is no limit to what you can achieve.

> **Student:** *What's it take to reach this understanding?*
>
> **Teacher:** *It begins with a small but compelling desire to understand it.*

In this book, you've looked at many ways to transform WOE into WOW. Every time you transform WOE into WOW, you transform desperation into elation and you see how your mistaken self-opinions have stopped you from being all you can be. This transformation causes a remarkable explosion of desire to understand the ultimate truth about yourself. And now you have it:

I am a rich and majestic child of infinite intelligence. I am marvelously made, and destined to win at whatever I set my mind to, and I am worthy of all that is good and beautiful.

YES, that's you! Perhaps you're surprised at how easy it is to understand something as profound as this Ultimate Understanding. Is it possible that understanding your marvelously made nature is as simple as reading this book and successfully completing the exercises? Need it be any more complicated than this?

There is an ancient story about Namaan, the commander of the army of the king of Aram. He was a highly regarded chivalrous soldier who was afflicted with leprosy. When he went to the prophet Elisha for advice, Elisha told him to wash seven times in the Jordan. Namaan was angered; he wanted more pomp and circumstance; he expected a much more elaborate solution to his affliction.

Let's look at this Ultimate Understanding again. Speak these words slowly. Speak them with full meaning in your voice. Listen to the words with mindfulness, not just with your rigid intellect. Sing the words from the heart until you feel their tantalizing allure. Let it be easy. Don't complicate it.

I AM A RICH AND MAJESTIC CHILD OF
INFINITE INTELLIGENCE.

I AM MARVELOUSLY MADE, AND DESTINED
TO WIN AT WHATEVER I SET MY MIND TO,
AND I AM WORTHY OF ALL THAT IS
GOOD AND BEAUTIFUL.

This understanding hums with winning promises. All efforts to understand this Ultimate Understanding strengthen you. When you fully understand how marvelously made you are, you begin thinking with an astonishingly agile mind. This is the condition of mind in which the mind works at its mighty best. You access natural powers that would have seemed supernatural to you before you came to this Ultimate Understanding.

When you understand this revelation, you can see why you could never solve your problems in the world. It's because you'd not solved your problems with yourself. You are doing this now.

Be glad when this understanding lifts you to a higher plateau of perception. It reveals things very different from what your mind even now conceives about you. Feel the rightness of what you are reading.

Are you ready to take the Ultimate Understanding deeper? Are you ready to place it in the deep-level thinking part of your mind where your true power lies? The subconscious is ready to listen to you and is ready to change standing orders that it received decades ago from childhood NO's. However, it can only do this if you communicate this understanding to it with simplicity and clarity.

Simplicity and clarity lead to deeper understanding, and deeper understanding leads to pure knowing. Pure knowing is a profound state of being that leads to unshakeable beliefs. This can only occur at the subconscious level of the mind.

So, let's break this Ultimate Understanding into its four simple parts, so you can communicate it effectively to the subconscious.

Four parts

I once read that to truly succeed in life, one must acquire as much knowledge as he can about what is right about himself. This is what you've been doing as you read this book, and you are now examining what is absolutely right about yourself.

There are four parts of this Ultimate Understanding, and you have prepared your mind to accept them. You have removed everything that could block acceptance of the truth.

When you give any one of the four parts of this understanding your special attention, you begin feeling comfortable with the other parts. Take a moment now and whisper each part to yourself while pausing and taking a breath between each part.

I am a rich and majestic child of infinite intelligence. I am marvelously made, and destined to win at whatever I set my mind to, and I am worthy of all that is good and beautiful.

Have no concern if you're having difficulty accepting any of the four parts. By simply opening to the possibility that all four parts are true, you allow remarkable changes to begin happening within you. Let's begin with examining the first part of this Ultimate Understanding.

Part I - Rich and majestic child

I AM A RICH AND MAJESTIC CHILD
OF INFINITE INTELLIGENCE.

I AM A RICH AND MAJESTIC CHILD
OF INFINITE INTELLIGENCE.

I AM A RICH AND MAJESTIC CHILD
OF INFINITE INTELLIGENCE.

Speak it. Sing it. Chant this first part of the Ultimate Understanding. Improvise and dance while chanting the words. Have fun with it. There is no wrong way of speaking it. The objective is to let the meaning vibrate through you.

It's a fabulous feeling to understand that you are a rich and majestic child of infinite intelligence. There is mental magic that comes with this understanding. You feel free to respond to your life circumstances in new and innovative ways. You no longer feel hindered by or compelled to react from past habits.

Understanding that you are a rich and majestic child of infinite intelligence attunes your mind to Universal Mind, that vast field of intelligence that pervades everything. This attunement awakens you to the presence of your limitless essence. Your mind is always mingling with Universal Mind, but you tuned it out when you tuned in to the NO's.

The infinite intelligence of Universal Mind is your source of incalculable wisdom and truth. This intelligence is omnipresent; it is as available as the next breath of air that you take. When you feel insecure, separate and alone, you look down at the mud, rather than up at the stars, and you deny yourself access to it. In other words, you tuned out when you created and identified with the *Counterfeit Self.*

When you understand that you are a rich and majestic child of infinite intelligence, you cannot help but feel whole and complete. There is something extraordinarily appealing about being receptive to this endless reservoir of enlightening knowledge. Would you agree?

Infinite intelligence never interferes with your choices. You are born with free will. You are born free to be whomever you choose to be and do whatever you choose to do. The more you follow your natural tendency to be authentic, the more you tune in to this intelligence.

When the mind of man is receptive to this field of intelligence, and remains receptive, the world has a Galileo, a da Vinci, an Einstein, a Stephen Hawking.

Great achievers and great thinkers make a habit of tuning in to infinite intelligence. This multiplies their intellectual capacity. Einstein spoke of receiving ideas that seemed to come from nowhere.

You know what's it's like to tune in to Universal Mind. When you have intuitive hunches, and you respond to life from these hunches, solving problems becomes remarkably easy, doesn't it. That's because you've tuned in to this intelligence.

Any time you sensitize your mind to receive the intelligence of Universal Mind, the vast mind of which your mind is always a part, you find your action has no contradictions. You are a rich and majestic child of infinite intelligence.

Rejoice when this understanding reveals something very different from what you believe about yourself right now.

Take ten minutes to absorb the fact that you are a rich

and majestic child of infinite intelligence. Ponder it. Reflect on it. What does this mean to you? One of the greatest moments in anyone's life is when he reacquaints himself with this child.

The next time you hear yourself saying that it's impossible to overcome a difficulty in your life, stop and say, *"Impossible? Not so! I'm possible … therefore it's possible."* The 'I' that you are referring to is the self that is a rich and majestic child of infinite intelligence. This self sees no difficulty as impossible to overcome.

> **Student:** *What happens when I transform the word 'impossible' to 'I'm possible,' and think of myself as a rich and majestic child of infinite intelligence?*
>
> **Teacher:** *You open your eyes to infinite possibilities.*

When you truly understand that you're a rich and majestic child of infinite intelligence, you feel an awe-inspiring higher force stir deep inside of you. Sing out this truth one more time, seeking to deepen your understanding: ***I am a rich and majestic child of infinite intelligence.*** Are you feeling it?

It is time to move on to part II:

Part II - Marvelously made

I am marvelously made.

I am marvelously made.

I am marvelously made.

Shout these words joyfully. Sing them gleefully and dance to the message. Throw your hands in the air, allowing the uplifting message to conquer any lower opinions that try to interrupt you.

Yearn to learn more and more about what it means to be marvelously made. You were born into this world with a mind that is fully equipped to change your world at will. This is a big part of your marvelously made nature. Understanding this one aspect of your marvelously made self enables you to act with full presence of this mind. This inspires you to concentrate your powers of mental attention on worthy objectives.

Might I say again, if you are going to be self-conscious, the *marvelously made self* is the *self* of which to be conscious. This is the *Authentic Self*. Life is lived with a lot less strain when you understand the true nature of being a human being.

The supreme reason for being here is to experience your marvelously made self with your marvelous talents and marvelous potential. Make it a habit to hunger and thirst for a better understanding of this.

Remind yourself every day that you are marvelously made. Write it on a card and leave it in the bathroom near your toothbrush. Read it every time you brush. You will find yourself even flossing with greater zeal.

The human being with which most folks are familiar is a being that is far from feeling marvelous. Have you ever considered trying something that looked difficult, and thought, *"Impossible, I'm only human; even considering this task feels overwhelming."* ?

The next time you catch yourself feeling overwhelmed by a task that seems impossible, stop and say (once again), *"Impossible? Not so! I'm possible ... therefore it's possible."* The 'I' that you are referring to is the marvelously made self. This self sees no task as overwhelming, no challenge as impossible to accomplish.

You are now taking time to acknowledge and appreciate the 'I' that exists beyond your usual assessment of being human. When you feel true appreciation, a higher way of seeing humanity and a better way of responding to life exists. Are you beginning to understand?

> **Student:** *What happens when I understand that I am marvelously made?*

> **Teacher:** *You end intimidation because the* Counterfeit Self *can no longer browbeat you.*

When you identify with your marvelously made nature, an awe-inspiring higher force stirs deep inside of you, which is exactly what you feel when you understand that you are a rich and majestic child of infinite intelligence. Now chant this part of the Ultimate Understanding one more time, seeking to deepen your understanding: ***I am marvelously made.*** Are you feeling it?

It is time to move on to part III.

PART III - DESTINED TO WIN

I AM DESTINED TO WIN AT WHATEVER I SET MY MIND TO.

I AM DESTINED TO WIN AT WHATEVER I SET MY MIND TO.

I AM DESTINED TO WIN AT WHATEVER I SET MY MIND TO.

Sing this declaration of truth with a vibrato tone. Have fun. Declare it with a foreign accent. Laughingly speak the words; speak them slowly, clearly articulating every syllable while releasing confidence into your tone. Persist until you have abandoned any sense of doubt that may grip you. That's it.

When you understand this part of the Ultimate Understanding, you know that your successes and failures are not accidents. When you act out of this understanding, you totally immerse yourself in what you're doing, and your action is complete.

You win at winning when you set your mind to winning, and you win at losing when you set your mind to losing, even if unconsciously. You no longer feel like a victim of circumstance when you understand the third part of the Ultimate Understanding. When you understand this part, you know the unchallengeable truth – winning or losing at the game of life is up to you.

Unfortunately, after hearing 60,000 NO's, we sabotage our potential for winning by setting our mind to feeling incompetent in 60,000 different ways. Thus, we set our sights on losing, and we 'win' at losing.

Own all of your successes. "There is no thought in any mind, but it quickly tends to convert itself into a power, and organize a huge instrumentality of means." - Emerson.

Now that you are communicating with all levels of your mind and you've learned to deny the lies, you will find, less and less, that you unconsciously set your mind to losing when attempting to succeed.

Your life is made and unmade by you. You are a marvelously made being. You have the capacity to express your marvelous qualities in a thousand different ways every day. This is your birthright. When you understand this, it's easy to set your mind to winning in a thousand different ways every day. Now you understand all that you need to know to succeed in life.

The news media will insist that you cannot avoid being a victim of circumstance, just read the paper or watch the evening news. The next time you hear yourself saying, *"Impossible, the circumstances are against me,"* stop and say, *"Impossible? Not so! I'm possible …therefore it's possible."* The 'I' that you are referring to is the self that is destined to win at whatever you set your mind to. This self sees itself as the maker of circumstances, not the victim of circumstances. This self knows that it is very capable of changing unsuitable circumstances.

> **Student:** *What's the best way to view troublesome circumstances?*
>
> **Teacher:** *All you need do is remember that you are destined to win at whatever you set your mind to, and this understanding will give you the right view.*

When you understand that you are destined to win at whatever you set your mind to, an awe-inspiring higher force stirs deep inside of you. Yes, the same feeling you feel when you understand that you are a rich and majestic child, which is the same feeling you feel when you understand that you are marvelously made. Simplicity heightens understanding, doesn't it. Now speak this truth one more time, seeking to deepen your understanding: *I am destined to win at whatever I set my mind to.* Are you feeling it?

And now, a look at the final part of the Ultimate Understanding.

Part IV - Worthy

I AM WORTHY OF ALL THAT IS
GOOD AND BEAUTIFUL.

I AM WORTHY OF ALL THAT IS
GOOD AND BEAUTIFUL.

I AM WORTHY OF ALL THAT IS
GOOD AND BEAUTIFUL.

Find a full-length mirror. Stand in front of it and look yourself right in the eyes. Stand as a person stands who knows that he is worthy of all that is good and beautiful. Point to yourself while speaking this affirmation; speak it with a convincing tone. Now whisper it.

Dare to listen to yourself as you affirm that you are worthy. With earnest listening comes a remarkably eager condition. Understanding your worthiness makes you eager to get on with your life.

Open your heart to this part of the Ultimate Understanding. You have all the knowledge you need to intellectually acknowledge your worthiness but you must *feel* it if you're to truly understand it. An ounce of feeling is more valuable than a ton of intellectualizing.

If you are to live for yourself, you must feel for yourself. At this very moment, you are creating your tomorrow with what you feel about yourself today.

You develop a magnetic personality when you feel at home with this part of the understanding; people flock to you. That's because you are free to be yourself, the *Authentic Self*. This self has an inner compass that guides you to the right responses in every situation.

All that you do outwardly is an expression of what you feel inwardly. From now on, let the feeling of worthiness be on your side. Feeling unworthy is a flawed feeling. The beginning of understanding your value is the end of useless struggling that comes from flawed feelings.

You are at the point where nothing can stop you from experiencing life's bountiful beauty. You have won the battle with WOE. There is no reason to be shy when asking for more from life. If you were a millionaire, would you ask for a penny? You are a millionaire in a million different ways. Moreover, you will experience a million enriching joys that life has in store for you when you appreciate your worth. Understand this right now – it is pure gold.

When you feel worthy, you project prosperity. A consciousness of prosperity prohibits the mechanical 'poor me' personality from expressing. The results are extraordinary.

With feeling worthy comes the feeling of self-fondness. When you feel fondness for yourself, you feel fondness for all of humanity. It all begins on the inside. Self-fondness inspires you to engage in interesting conversations that bring out the best in others. That's because you see them as valuable and feel fond of them, which is a direct consequence of seeing yourself as valuable and feeling fond of yourself.

What better way to help others help themselves, and what better way to help your children help themselves, than to see their worthiness and help them see it? You are not only able to help your generation, you are able to help the next generation by simply feeling worthy and wanting to spread the word.

The real reward comes in knowing that you lift yourself to a higher plateau of living by helping others lift themselves. Life would be dull if we didn't do nice things for one another; it's one of the more gladdening parts of the journey.

Beware, the trap – 'you shouldn't have'. Have you ever caught yourself saying, "*Oh shucks, you shouldn't have*," when someone does something nice for you? As humble as it may sound, this statement offers a woeful perspective. It implies that you are unworthy of such niceness. Don't exhaust your feeling of worthiness in order to be humble. Simply say, "*Thank you! This is very generous of you.*" I hope you're nodding in understanding of this tip.

Anytime you hear yourself saying, "*Impossible, I'll never be that fortunate,*" about an experience you'd love to have, stop and say, "*Impossible? Not so! I'm possible, therefore it's possible.*" The 'I' that you are referring to is the self that is worthy of all that is good and beautiful. This self anticipates good fortune.

Student: *Won't people think I'm self-centered if I say I'm worthy of all that's good and beautiful?*

Teacher: *Stay away from anyone who says you are not worthy.*

When you understand that you are worthy of all that is good and beautiful, I imagine you know what happens next: an awe-inspiring higher force stirs inside of you. Now whisper this truth one more time, seeking to deepen your understanding: *I am worthy of all that is good and beautiful.* Are you feeling it?

TRUE HELP COMES

As mentioned earlier, true help comes when you understand any part of this Ultimate Understanding. Understanding one part reinforces the other parts. Understanding that you are a rich and majestic child attracts good and beautiful things into your life, which reinforces the understanding that you are a valuable and worthy human being.

Understanding that you are marvelously made, makes it easy to understand that you are destined to win at

whatever you set your mind to. When you understand any part of this Ultimate Understanding, you
abandon opinions and painful memories that prevent
you from understanding any of the other parts.

With this Ultimate Understanding comes a feeling
of supreme optimism. You no longer fear the disap-
proval or discouraging remarks of others and you no
longer feel the urge to disapprove of or offer discouraging remarks to others.

With a supreme feeling of optimism, you do not
feel inferior, nor do you feel superior to others. This
is because your new understanding about yourself
becomes your understanding about everyone. Life
becomes a warm and inviting journey. The rewards you receive in healthy and harmonious
relationships are immeasurable.

Imagine looking at everyone, no matter what his
station in life, and understanding that he is a rich and
majestic child of infinite intelligence. Now you see
humanity as it truly is.

Make a conscious effort to tell the truth about yourself to yourself daily. Work with the Ultimate Under-

standing until you experience a new kind of mood, vastly superior to any mood that you now consider a valuable mood. There is no better way to make the mind intelligent to your superior nature than through repetition and 'acting as though' it is so.

When this understanding reigns supreme in your whole mind, you will never go back and live in the world as you did before.

You have always done the best you could, given what you believed about yourself. However, you can never do your best until you understand what is true about you. Consider this understanding a spiritual awakening that is correcting all misunderstandings that you hold about yourself and others.

> *This understanding is a spiritual awakening; it corrects all misunderstandings that you hold about yourself and others.*

If you endure in your pursuit to understand, you will be sure to understand, and your mind will become a vessel into which will pour ever more inspiring understandings.

True understanding goes beyond ideology. True understanding is pure knowing. When pure knowing of your marvelously made nature illuminates your consciousness, it's easy to reclaim your originality.

When the knowing is pure, that you are marvelously made, your friends will say, *"Wow you've changed, you used to be nervous (or shy ... or quick to anger)."* And you will say, *"That ME doesn't live here anymore."*

ONE MORE TIME

Let's say this together one more time.

I AM A RICH AND MAJESTIC CHILD OF INFINITE INTELLIGENCE.

I AM MARVELOUSLY MADE, AND DESTINED TO WIN AT WHATEVER I SET MY MIND TO, AND I AM WORTHY OF ALL THAT IS GOOD AND BEAUTIFUL.

If you've completed this book and done the exercises, you're ready to take your *Second Chance at Success*, and have already begun to succeed. You've brought the forces of your personal evolution under your control.

From now on, be your own rich bounty. Until we meet again, enjoy the bliss of understanding.

R O A R

What's next?

You've completed the first of my Trilogy of Truths. Each book guides you to higher perceptions that enable you to subdue conditioned thought-habits. You've taken the time to resolve problems that come with 60,000 NO's. You've awakened to the brilliant truth of your unlimited potential and you now have the Ultimate Understanding.

What happens next, after you have passed through the dark period of WOE? What happens when you're free of tensions that come with NO? What happens next is an astonishing period of growth and development. You find yourself in a state of breathless anticipation of your future.

The work you've done prepares you for a superb life. You've begun to understand the process of your psychological development, and this knowledge enables you to determine the speed of your future psychological evolution.

Your personality reflects the degree to which your psychology has evolved, and your experiences are a reflection of your mental illumination. There is a treasure in every person, and it is really quite fantastic when you discover the treasure in you.

A remarkable benefit of psychological growth is that you are increasingly unaffected by negative events, and that's because you obtain much more happiness from being your natural self than you do when you try to obtain it from your environment.

Are you ready to hold yourself accountable for your psychological development? Are you willing to abolish the left over habits that remain after completing Book One – those persistent habits that prevent you from consciously choosing the "I AM" that you desire to be? To do this is to experience your highest destiny.

Your highest destiny is to consciously choose the "I AM" that you desire to be.

In Book Two you will learn how to be a brilliant source of ideas that quicken your psychological development. There is nothing more interesting and practical than using your mind to optimize your resources so that you take command of your psychological evolution.

When you hold yourself accountable for your evolutionary progress, you evolve from being 'just me', a person who settles for mediocrity, to being an innovative thinker who seeks excellence in everything you do. This is the decisive expression of human dignity.

Our genetic evolution is peaking

I believe the genetic evolution of human beings is peaking. Our bodies have evolved over hundreds of thousands of years. Nature has bestowed upon us many incredible physical advantages.

These physical advantages include opposable thumbs and a highly developed brain and protruding jaw structure that enable us to communicate in a way that is both efficient and profound. We are able to use the synergy created by the combination of our intelligence and our physicality in ways that far surpass all other creatures on the planet. We can pretty much adapt to any environment.

> **Student:** *So what's left if our physical evolution is peaking?*

> **Teacher:** *What's left is our psychological evolution.*

I believe that we are spiritual beings, whole and complete just as we are, but we are taught that we are much less than that. I believe that we are playing a game of hide-and-seek with ourselves. We hide our Authentic Selves deep inside by convincing ourselves that we are incomplete and limited in countless ways.

As we go through the period of 60,000 NO's, we create a Counterfeit Self to hide behind. We hide the truth about our potential from ourselves and consequently, we no longer feel whole and complete.

Is it possible that you took physical form to play the game of hide-and-seek with yourself? Is it possible that the sublime experience that you are seeking comes when you recover the original powers that you lost by mistakenly assuming that you are something less than a spiritual being with unlimited potential? Is it possible that you came to this planet where opposites exist to experience the truth of your *unlimitedness?*

Humpty Dumpty sat on a wall. Humpty Dumpty had a great fall. All the King's horses and all the King's men couldn't put Humpty together again. No one could put Humpty together again … except Humpty!

Perhaps Humpty was like you and I – perhaps he was knocked off the wall with 60,000 NO's. And no one could help Humpty recover his original powers except himself. No one can do this for you, except YOU. I will show you how in Book Two.

I believe that we put ourselves in touch with our whole and complete spiritual selves again by holding ourselves accountable for our own psychological evolution. When you hold yourself accountable, you undergo a self-transformation that recovers your original powers and heightens your spiritual experiences of *self*.

This language may sound esoteric, but it is really very practical. Taking charge of your own psychological evolution is crucial to experiencing those praiseworthy aspirations that are important to you.

Book Two teaches you a practice that will quicken your psychological evolution and increase your experiences of *self* as a spiritual being.

Abstractions

Your highly developed brain has evolved to the point where you are able to create inspiring abstractions and act upon them with a conviction to make them real.

When you are able to increase the level of your abstractions and freely choose how you respond to conditions in your life, you will have the power to abolish limiting opinions and surpass your old reactions in extraordinary ways.

Your capacity to elevate your abstractions and act on them in a productive manner distinguishes you as a member of the superior species on the planet.

The concept of abstraction may be new to you. An abstraction is simply an idea or synthesis of ideas that develops from your musings, reveries and daydreams. There are ways of increasing your level of abstraction by elevating your consciousness to loftier heights – such as meditation, contemplation, positive ruminations and repeated affirmations.

An abstraction is an idea or synthesis of ideas that develops out of your musings, reveries and daydreams.

Hear this magnificent message! There is another way – a simple, joyful and effective way – to increase your level of abstractions. If you resolutely practice the method that I offer in Book Two, you will not only master the ability to increase your level of abstractions, you will also learn how to transmute them into inspiring visions that quicken dynamic action.

You have a role to play

This is an extraordinary time in your life. Human evolution is advancing metaphysically, and you can participate. You can consciously reach beyond your 'just me' self and make empowering choices befitting your noble nature.

 You have a role to play in the psychological evolution of humanity. You play your role well when you treasure new aspirations that come with your elevated abstractions.

Placing yourself in charge of your psychological evolution enriches your experience of human dignity, which contributes to the dignity of all humanity.

You have access to an unlimited supply of energy and

you use it wisely when you learn to blend intuition and practical effort while acting on your abstractions. Book Two teaches you this blending process. Mastering this will offer you rarified experiences that give you clear reminders of your spiritual essence.

Now that you've had a glimpse at who you truly are, can you feel the pride that comes with holding yourself accountable for your psychological evolution?

Your highest responsibility

The authentic you knows that you are destined for great things and knows what's most important for you to experience. After completing Book One, you understand that you are worthy of all that is good and beautiful. As you read Book Two, it will become apparent to you that increasing your experience of human dignity is your highest responsibility.

When you take your highest responsibility to heart and learn to love it with your whole mind, soul, and strength, you give yourself a breath-taking treasure – an attitude that increases your capacity for pure enjoyment in everything you do.

The game of life is honest. When you awaken your dozing energy and give all of yourself to the game, you experience greater levels of ability to succeed with whatever you set your mind to.

Self-honesty

Self-honesty offers extraordinary power. Accept right now that you have the capacity to bring perfect order to any disorder that remains in your psychology. Accept that you have the power to put an end to what is stopping you from experiencing the sublime joy of human dignity. By accepting these facts, you avoid traps set by others. Book Two proves that self-honesty is always the warmest, friendliest, and most positive choice that you can make.

You were inspired to read Book One by your desire to reach beyond your 'just me' personality and place yourself in the winner's circle of life. This desire drives you to contemplate even higher experiences of self.

The power to achieve your ideals has always been with you and you now know that any attempt to find this power outside of you is always in vain.

Book Two shows you how to direct your power in ways that guarantee evolutionary progress in the psychological domain. As you progress in this domain you enjoy greater success in all domains of living.

Make it your mission to consciously participate in your psychological evolution, and the qualities of nobility and decency will become supreme forces in your life. You live productively and peacefully when you accept these supreme forces as part of you.

So now let's get to the main event of Book Two – learning to ROAR. When you learn to ROAR with skill, you activate your mind to consistently produce noble and valuable results.

ROAR

When enslaved by echoing NO's, you could not possibly understand your role as an evolving being. You would not have believed that you could elevate your abstractions and refine your actions to experience yourself as a spiritual being.

No matter how much you've lulled yourself with protestations of NO, you always have higher guidance available, which you will clearly hear when you learn to ROAR.

ROAR is my acronym for:

 Recognize yourself as a marvelously made being with the power to design your destiny.

 **Organize** your self-talk to reinforce this recognition.

 **Absorb** this recognition deep into your subconscious.

 **Realize** this recognition in your life.

ROAR-ing offers unique power. It helps you rule all experiences in your life by the power of your mind.

When you ROAR effectively, you draw upon intuitive intelligence to guide you. Intuitive intelligence inspires practical effort and productive behavior that lifts you high above the reactive state of fear. You no longer get caught in exterior confusion.

You gain control of your progress with personal effort. ROAR-ing rejects all harmful influences that stop you from making the effort. You recover your original powers to create your life as you dream it can be when you learn to ROAR about your unlimited nature.

Are you ready to join?

Come! Join the troupe of ROAR-ers. Come! Join the community of awakening human beings. Become a great observer. Exercise your prerogative to experience your *Power of Conscious Selection*. To do this, you must think clearly, not from muddled abstractions. This is what ROAR-ers do.

ROAR-ing may clash with your old ways, but you will gladly sacrifice the old in order to pursue the new that comes when you exercise your *Power of Conscious Selection*.

Are you ready to take charge of your transformation? Are you ready to design your destiny so your life unfolds as you want it to be? You achieve these things and more when you learn to ROAR.

Understanding that you are a rich and majestic child of infinite intelligence is pure abstraction. Yet, with this abstraction, a new star of truth burns zealously in your mind – it is your turn to return home to your spiritual nature.

You cannot weigh or measure the incredible abstractions you can create with the Ultimate Understanding that you've gained in Book One. These abstractions have no physical volume; even the finest of scientific instruments cannot detect them. Yet, when you inspire yourself with abstractions like the Ultimate Understanding and transform them into action, you break free of any hard shell of negativity that still encases you. You find yourself living in a new world that is beautiful beyond description – like the chick that breaks out of its hard shell.

It is written in the King James Bible, *"Where there is no vision, the people shall perish."* Upon completion of Book Two, you will have visions of a life that you will cherish. You will feel honored to hold yourself accountable for your psychological evolution. You will look deeply into your difficulties and see wonderful opportunities to advance your progress.

Upon completion of Book Two, you will value the experience of human dignity above all else and you will know that something new and fabulous is just ahead of you.

We focus on the same goal

Fundamentally, everyone focuses on the same goal – to sweep away all restrictions that stop us from living sensibly and happily. We aspire never again to be careless of our personal welfare.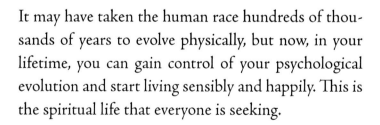

It may have taken the human race hundreds of thousands of years to evolve physically, but now, in your lifetime, you can gain control of your psychological evolution and start living sensibly and happily. This is the spiritual life that everyone is seeking.

Book Two furthers your efforts to purify your mind and rid your behavior of all the residue that lingers from old NO's. When the mind is purified, you are conscious of the self that is pure. When your consciousness is right, no person or event has the power to harm your soaring spirit.

You have an amazing capacity for creative self-management and psychological growth. Act on this truth and nothing will stop you from shining as bright as a flaming supernova.

I will see you soon, with Book Two.

We at the Mind Adventure Company whole-heartedly support those who are dedicated to experiencing the best of themselves. Mind Adventure, Inc., is committed to helping you awaken to the truth about your incredible potential as a human being and to give you the tools to experience this truth. We offer seminars, workshops, speeches, webinars, blogs, a blog radio show, books and specific programs that help you live from your superlatively creative nature. At Mind Adventure, we love to say with bright smiles on our faces, if it *ain't* practical – it *ain't* spiritual. This reminds us that a successful life journey is a spiritual journey, and a spiritual journey requires practical common sense. The knowledge we share presents great truths of the ages in ways that are easy to understand and are useful in your daily affairs.

www.mindadventure.com

CPSIA information can be obtained at www.ICGtesting.com
Printed in the USA
BVOW082348090812

297540BV00006B/1/P

9 780980 229943